Be Bullish on Life and
Win Big!!

[signature]

Travis' coaching prowess shines through in his latest book, The 3 CEOs. *This book was written for financial advisors who are passionate and driven. It will help advisors fine-tune their businesses during a period of unprecedented change in our industry. An excellent read for those who are willing to take the necessary steps to change, and as a result, maximize growth in their businesses and experience an impactful life.*

—JOSEPH S. DE SENA, CFP®, MBA
FORBES BEST-IN-STATE WEALTH ADVISOR

The three keys to a successful self-help book are a willing learner, a knowledgeable experienced teacher, and information that is actionable by most readers. The 3 CEOs *hits the trifecta. The teacher has appeared. It is Travis Chaney. His teaching, coaching and mentoring expertise is well documented. This book is not about Travis. It is about the future you. Either you decide to continue working 'IN the business' full time or you decide to carve out time to work 'ON the business'. 'When the student is ready the teacher will appear.' Are you ready?*

—STEVE BARGER,
INDUSTRY DISRUPTOR SINCE 1978

THE 3CEOs

The Three Most Important Roles Entrepreneurial Financial Advisors Play

TRAVIS RAY CHANEY

Foreword by Dr. Nido R. Qubein, President, High Point University

Dynamic Directions - D2, Inc. | Owensboro, KY

Published by
Dynamic Directions-D2, Inc. | Owensboro, KY

Publisher's Cataloging-in-Publication Data
Chaney, Travis Ray.

The 3 CEOs : the three most important roles entrepreneurial financial advisors play / by Travis Ray Chaney. – Owensboro, KY : Dynamic Directions–D2, Inc., 2022.

p. ; cm.

ISBN13: 978-0-9601087-0-1

Chief executive officers. 2. Executive ability. 3. Success in business. I. Title.

HD38.2.C43 2022
658.42--dc23

Project coordination by Jenkins Group, Inc. | www.jenkinsgroupinc.com

Cover design by John Barnett
Interior design by Brooke Camfield

Printed in the United States of America
25   24   23   22   21   •   5   4   3   2   1

Contents

Foreword

I've been Travis Chaney's business coach for almost two decades, and I'm proud of his many achievements. Quite a few of the concepts he relates in this book are strategies and systems I've been teaching to entrepreneurial leaders for many years, and I've encouraged him to share these concepts with you in this book.

The appreciated difference with Travis is he listens, learns, adapts, applies, and improves ideas he encounters with professional precision.

That's why he is in such demand to guide and mentor others. As the CEO of Dynamic Directions, a coaching and consulting firm focused on building an extraordinary life and practice for financial advisors, Travis and his team have won a number of awards in recent years. In fact, in the past six out of ten years, the firm's coaches have won the Coach of the Year award from the top five, nationally ranked broker-dealer they work with. (Travis has personally won the award three times, and three of the coaches he mentors have also won the award.)

He has also helped several clients win such prestigious awards as Barron's Top 1,200, Barron's Top 100 Women Advisors, Forbes Best in State, The Financial Times Top 400 Advisors, and many others.

These results show that what you hold in your hands isn't merely a book. It's a roadmap to success in your business and a step-by-step compass to significance in your life.

As president of High Point University, I work diligently at planting seeds of greatness in the minds, hearts, and souls of our students. We are preparing them for the world as it is going to be, not as it is or as it was. Life skills are a prerequisite to enjoying a life of purpose and accomplishment.

This book is laden with life skills and business acumen. Read it to learn. Apply it to enhance your lot in life.

When all is said and done, the two most important words in the English language are influence and impact: how you influence others and what impact you leave behind.

In his work and in his life, Travis is focused on creating for his friends and colleagues a circle of influence and an avalanche of meaningful impact.

I'm proud of him as an author, speaker, consultant, teacher, and friend.

Nido R. Qubein
President, High Point University
Executive Chairman, Great Harvest Bread Company
Board Member, Truist, La–Z–Boy Corporation, nThrive
Author, two dozen books and audio programs

Introduction

Golf legend Bobby Jones used to say that competitive golf is played on a five-and-a-half-inch course: the space between your ears.

The game of life is played on that same course. How well you do, how far you go, how fulfilled you feel, all depends on keeping your head in the game.

As a business coach and consultant, I've seen the Bobby Jones principle proven correct again and again. I have coached many people who succeed beyond their wildest dreams, overcoming all kinds of obstacles, thanks to the way they play the game between their ears. And I know others who feel frustrated that they've never quite reached their full potential, because they have never achieved the mental discipline of staying out of their own way.

The difference between these two outcomes is what this book is all about.

Every business leader among the scores I've coached was already very successful by most standards when we began to work together. The ones who have since succeeded most spectacularly, however, were those who did much more than learn new roles, new tactics, and new skills. They were the ones who did the hard work of making a serious shift in their mindset, away from past beliefs and attitudes and toward their new future.

Taking your business to the next level begins in your head. *You must* know who you are and what you stand for. You must know what you believe and just how far you will go to support that belief. Belief alone is not enough, of course. You must follow through with goals, strategies, tactics, and execution. But if you attempt to get to a new level with your old way of thinking, all those new goals, strategies, and tactics will ultimately disappoint in their execution.

You can go online right now and download a list of the top fifty-seven bright ideas and techniques that promise to make you six figures in six weeks. You can try some or all of them, and a few might actually give you a bump in sales this month or the next.

The question is how many of those fifty-seven ideas you will still be trying a month from now. Or a year from now. Not many. They're just not sustainable. Silver-bullet solutions never work for long, if they ever work at all, because attempting new behaviors with old ways of thinking is all just wasted effort. It's like planting seeds in barren soil.

The reason is as simple as A, B, C.

A. Your results are determined by your behaviors.

B. Your behaviors are directed by your beliefs.

C. In order to change your results, you must first change your beliefs.

Beliefs → Behaviors → Results

It's simple logic. You might have learned it in sixth grade. Yet many people don't recognize this and spend countless hours trying to change their behaviors while holding steadfastly to their prior beliefs.

Introduction

You picked this book up for a reason. Maybe you're stuck at your current level and can't figure out how to move higher. Maybe you're not sure how to motivate your team. Perhaps you doubt the direction of your next marketing campaign. Maybe you're not even sure why you're doing what you're doing. The hours you spend lying awake in the dark are not helping.

This book will help you, but only if you're ready to gear up and take a long, deep dive into your business and into your entire life. Why? Because it works, and because it's worth building an extraordinary life and business. So many of the advisors who have been coached through this process have exceeded their original business goals by several magnitudes of success, all because they did the difficult work of rethinking and reframing beliefs that some of them had had since early childhood.

More than a few advisors have told me that our process felt like a spiritual awakening. In the end, that's really what we're trying to provide our clients: forging a new connection with the spirit inside them that motivates them each day to be their very best.

Don't get me wrong. Our clients don't come to us for behavioral therapy or spiritual guidance. They come to us because they want better results. They want to grow their top line and their bottom line. They want more assets under management. They want more new money. They want more high-value clients. They expect us to coach them to be better and reach higher.

And we assure them we have plenty of strategies and tactics for them to try, proven techniques that will help them do all these things. But these concerns are secondary. The primary issue is this: Are you willing to put in the effort required to change? If you have a positive attitude and are willing to put in the effort, the results will take care of themselves.

THE THREE CEOS

In the coming pages you'll learn how to develop a clear vision for your future by examining all your beliefs, attitudes, values, and motivations. Then you'll be able to set measurable goals and focused action plans that are aligned with what you find most important and meaningful in life. From there you will have a powerful mental framework from which to think entrepreneurially and lead like a true CEO.

Every CEO serves three distinct leadership functions, which is why this book applies three distinct meanings to the CEO acronym. A CEO is a chief executive officer, of course, but a CEO is also a cultural excellence officer and a client experience officer. The best CEOs excel at all three of these functions, and the book is organized in three parts that correspond to each function.

Of the three CEO functions, the client experience officer comes last for the simple reason that developing the company's client experience is necessarily the final step. Until you know who you are as a chief executive officer, and until you know how to lead as a cultural excellence officer, you can't possibly conceive what kind of client is a fit with your plans and company culture. You must first map out a unique plan for growth that is aligned with your personal leadership vision and your company's cultural values. Only then can you develop an accurate profile of the the kind of client you want to attract and serve.

My previously published book, *Turbo Growth* (2010), is primarily focused on the professional development of the individual financial advisor. It encourages readers to see a bigger, brighter future for themselves, and to position their firms for breakout success based on industry best practices and real business experience. *Turbo Growth* coaches readers to discover purpose and meaning in their lives as the essential foundation for growing their businesses and shows how to practice the art of the possible.

Introduction

This book picks up where *Turbo Growth* leaves off, and it raises the stakes considerably. The three CEOs model challenges you to assume the three essential roles of entrepreneurial leadership as a chief executive capable of taking a large and growing business to heights you may have previously thought impossible. Through the three essential CEO functions in leading execution, culture, and client experience, the imperatives of turbo growth will show you how to accelerate your learning as you build a great business around what's most important to you in life. This book is aimed at fulfilling *Turbo Growth*'s promise of creating a great life for yourself, one filled with financial success, achievement, and significance.

In part 1, I'll look at the chief executive officer's role as the leader who casts the vision, sets the goals, and puts everybody on a path to get there. None of this will be accomplished very effectively if you haven't looked at your core beliefs and considered which of them have become fixed and self-limiting to some degree. So, in chapter 1, there are questionnaires and other self-assessments to help steer you toward a shift in your mindset, enabling you to rethink, reframe, and refocus your perceptions and arrive at a new vision for yourself and your business, propelling you forward.

Leading a fast-growing enterprise with dozens or hundreds of employees is an enormous responsibility. If you don't know the core beliefs that drive you as a leader, you risk endlessly searching for new and different solutions outside yourself. Rudderless, you can start going in circles. And because you're the leader, everyone in your organization will soon be going in circles right behind you.

In chapter 2, we'll move on to the rewards of risk, and discuss how rapid growth demands some choices and decisions that are inherently risky. There are many ways to be strategic and minimize risk. It is also important to consider that in this age of digital disruption, *not* taking risks and *not* changing with the times is likely the riskiest move of all. I will show you our process of intentional congruence, which helps you manage risk while taking on innovation and responding to disruptive competitive threats.

Earning, learning, and serving is the subject of chapter 3. When you take the long view of your business, when you know where you're going, you have a better idea of what's missing and you can make adjustments along the way. You learn to ask yourself what you intend to pass on at the end of your journey, and how that determines your day-to-day choices.

In part 2, you will learn about your role as a cultural excellence officer. Chapter 4 explores how your company culture is inevitably an extension of yourself and your values, your vision, and your sense of mission. Chapter 5 gets into how you must communicate and project culture among employees, clients, vendors, and other company stakeholders. Chapter 5 also stresses the importance of hiring for cultural fit.

A lot of the entrepreneurs we work with have become accustomed to working toward their goals and visions without writing out a plan. That won't work for a company that's planning a period of fast, scalable growth. Chapter 6 is about how to develop a ten-year plan that is powerful enough to imbue every team member with the company's values and culture. If this seems like a lot of work, it is a necessary stage in scaling your business. Consider how five-piece rock bands never need sheet music, but a 100-member symphony orchestra can't function without it.

With part 3, it's time to pull everything together as a client experience officer. Chapter 7 asks you to first position yourself and your personal behaviors in ways that are aligned with your company's objectives. Chapter 8 is about how to develop a client experience that's an expression of your authentic self and at the heart of your company's brand. Chapter 9 discusses ways to build a self-renewing, self-perpetuating client-referral culture that will sustain the growth of your business by attracting top-shelf clients you find truly rewarding to work with—and not just in financial terms. In the final chapter, you'll come to a choice about how you want to proceed in life. You can choose to live through your regrets, or you can choose to live through your dreams.

Some of the concepts I'll introduce along the way, such as intentional congruence, the product of the product, and transformational leadership, have been learned from my good friend and mentor Dr. Nido Qubein, the president of High Point University in North Carolina, who is also an accomplished entrepreneur. He is the former chairman of the Great Harvest Bread Company and serves on the boards of several national organizations, including Truist, formerly known as BB&T (a Fortune 500 company), the La-Z-Boy Corporation and Dots Stores. He also received The Ellis Island Medal of Honor (as did four US presidents) and The Horatio Alger Award for Distinguished Americans, and he has written more than two dozen books and audio programs distributed worldwide.

I've had the privilege of knowing Nido since 2005. Over the years, I've internalized so many of Nido's lessons and made them my own in so many ways that I'm not sure who I'd be if Nido had not taken me under his wing as a coaching client for the last fifteen years. As all great leaders are, Nido is first and foremost a *teacher*, and as his proud pupil, I consider this book to be a contribution to his substantial legacy.

YOUR BELIEFS DRIVE YOUR RESULTS

I am the CEO of Dynamic Directions (we also call it D2), a coaching and consulting firm focused on building an extraordinary life and practice for financial advisors. I began coaching years ago, after my own experience with coaching had propelled my practice's success to the point where I only had to work one week per month. Thanks to my coach's counseling and prodding, I'd streamlined my client list from 550 to just 140, while tripling my revenue, all in about two years. Today, what I ask of you in this book is no different from what I continue to expect from myself. I don't always succeed at the level I desire, and I don't always hit the goals I've set, but the focus and effort are there every day.

Our firm and our clients have won a number of awards in recent years. Those I'm most proud of are the ones that our clients have earned, because most of them have won for the first time while engaged with our firm.

Colleagues often ask me, "Jeez, what are you guys doing right?" and I always say the same thing: "First and foremost, we've picked the right people. Period."

First, we do our due diligence on new hires so all our team members are on the same page within our culture. Then we do even greater due diligence on prospective clients. We don't have a sales orientation in obtaining new clients. We have a client-fit orientation.

We invite prospective clients to interview us to see if we're a fit, but we also let them know that we're interviewing them to see if they're a fit with us. We show them our coaching process, step-by-step, and if it's not attractive to them, or if they're not really interested in going through one or more of our steps, we're happy to pass. We know we're not right for everyone.

By being selective in this way at D2, we end up working with clients who are truly committed to the coaching we offer. The average length of our client relationships with our comprehensive coaching and consulting approach is between six and seven years, far beyond the industry average of one or two years. For me, one of the most rewarding things is that I get to see our clients' dreams come true as they achieve results far beyond what they initially thought were possible.

Introduction

If you want to have a more successful, first-class, award-winning consulting practice, then in this book, I offer you the way you can achieve those goals. That's the three CEOs model. It starts with you. It has to.

That's also why some of the most important work in this book, the foundational work, is right in the first two chapters. I won't be warming you up or easing you into the subject matter. This book starts with some hard work, looking at your life, looking at your dreams, looking at your beliefs. There will be exercises you may feel like avoiding. Those are likely the most valuable to you personally, though they might lead you to acknowledge you've been doing some things wrong for many years, which is never easy to admit to yourself.

At those moments, I want you to remember why you picked up this book. You may suspect there are reasons why you are successful and yet still not successful *enough*. I've gone through this process with enough people over the years to know that the answer lies in your core beliefs, including some beliefs you may not even be aware of.

Later in the book, you're likely to be faced with some unpleasant choices you'd rather not make. Some of them may be choices you've been putting off for years because of your beliefs. Once you've raised your awareness of what it takes to get where you want to go, this book will spur you to take actions that can't be put off any longer, not if you want to grow and thrive.

Are you up for that? Are you willing to put in that effort? Are you ready to do the hard work required to change? Are you ready to *use* this book as intended: as a tool for life-changing transformation?

If not, I'd just as soon you put it down now. Give it away to someone who you think can use it. Because if you're planning to page through this book for pleasurable reading, or if you're tempted to graze on the ideas that seem most appealing to you, then this book is not for you.

There are thousands of other books out there offering easy silver-bullet solutions. You'll have no problem finding one you'll enjoy more than this one.

On the other hand, if you read this book carefully, if you do the exercises, if you mark it up and really *use* the book, I promise that you will start seeing positive results very soon. The process is designed around building early leverage and momentum so that the first rewards for your hard work will be recognizable fairly quickly.

I believe in the value of momentum. It is a true force multiplier when you can get it working in your favor. And then you're ready to deal with the other kind of momentum, which is not necessarily in your favor: the momentum of change. Simply put, change is hard.

Accelerated change is perhaps the only truly foreseeable future development in our industry, or in any other industry. It's coming, brought to your door by the marketplace, by your competition, by the government, by your clients. The only question is how you will deal with that change.

If you are governed more by sales than by culture, or more by tactics then strategy, change can be a terrible threat, one that sends you scrambling for new clients and smarter tactics. If, on the other hand, you are governed by a specific set of principles that underlie and guide everything you do, change is less likely to present you with an emergency. Strong strategies, backed by strong principles and a strong culture, are your bulwarks against the unforeseen, unimagined, and unwelcome.

The three CEOs model is designed to yield exponential results in the face of continual change and disruption. That's because all of this book's disciplines and exercises are based on eternal and unchanging principles that inform and enrich each other. Once your principles are clear, your choices will be clearer, even if they're not always the most attractive choices. A strong company culture will help you make the most of those choices, which in turn will earn you glowing referrals from your carefully cultivated client base.

The ultimate goal of the book is to help you live a more fulfilling life of purpose and service. You can make all the money in the world, but if you're not satisfied with the other areas of your life, what does it matter?

What you will find in this book is that most business lessons are also life lessons. Once you have your framework of personal principles in place, you will be more than merely poised for success in your field. You will be well on your way to becoming a better spouse, a better parent, a better friend, a better person.

There is a bigger, better life out there for you, and that's not something you get from the latest trick or tweak to increase your email response rate. A better life is something you get by looking inward first and reflecting on what's most important in life. For many who have gone through this process, it's been the greatest adventure imaginable.

PART ONE

The Chief Executive Officer

CHAPTER ONE

The Turbo-Growth Mindset

What are the differences between achievers and high achievers?

Why do some business owners attain escalated growth, seemingly without losing a step, while others need to scrape and scramble for every small percentage gain?

From what I've seen, high achievers have these four key characteristics in common:

1. **High achievers implement change at a rapid pace.** They maintain an enviable rhythm of continuous upward evolution within their companies. They choose a direction, a vision of the future, and then pursue it with conviction. And when they experience setbacks, they roll with the punches. They adapt to unforeseen circumstances and avoid the temptation to jettison their vision and plans.

2. **High achievers excel at managing risk.** They know that risks point the way to great rewards, so they take more risks than most people. Risk doesn't frighten them, but they're not foolhardy either. High achievers are skilled at assessing best- and worst-case scenarios. They determine their actions

according to how much risk they can tolerate, and how well they can soften the blow in the event of a bad outcome.

3. **High achievers leverage their resources.** They make the most of what they have. They maximize the use of their time and talent. They delegate tasks best done by their team members, and they empower their various team leaders to do the same. As the conductor of a symphony orchestra does, they create amazing results by directing the work of others.

4. **High achievers are decisive.** They confront problems head-on and focus on the solutions. They make choices quickly, and they stick by them. The same vision of the future that enables them to embrace constant change also allows them to see their choices more clearly, and to optimize the results of the choices they make.

It's hard to find a high-achieving individual who isn't proficient in all these areas. To achieve what I've called turbo growth, your engine needs to be hitting on all four of these cylinders. Misfiring on any one of them will reduce the power generated by the other three.

These four characteristics of high achievement are not among the competencies taught in business schools. There are courses offering instruction in theories of change management, risk management, decision science, leadership, and the like, but business school coursework won't turn you into a high achiever. I've met high achievers with nothing more than a high-school diploma, and I've met PhDs who have a knack for running businesses straight into the ground. Intellectual firepower and advanced knowledge are not among the secrets to high achievement.

What high achievers all have in common is what I call a turbo-growth mindset. They believe in themselves, they believe in their people, they believe in their mission. This mindset leads them to make choices aligned with their beliefs. They spend their time wisely. They hire people they believe in. They establish a vision of the future that everyone in their firms can believe in.

As Dr. Qubein teaches, the beliefs of these high achievers guide the firm's behavior, which drives results that reinforce beliefs. It is this turbo-growth mindset—one that aligns beliefs, behaviors, and results in a virtuous spiral—that spurs high achievers to success.

It's common for other entrepreneurs to try to model their behaviors on high achievers. They read inspiring profiles of people who have accomplished great things, and they try to replicate some of those people's best practices or learn from their strategic choices. What most people lack, unfortunately, is the mindset and set of beliefs that drive that behavior.

Think of the high achievers you've met or have admired from afar. You'll find very few of them are ever plagued by doubt. Why is that? Where do they get that resolve and self-confidence? It's almost impossible to say.

And it doesn't matter. That's the good news. You don't need any insights into the inner thoughts of Jeff Bezos, Warren Buffet, Steve Jobs, or any of the great business leaders commonly upheld as entrepreneurial role models. You only need to develop insights into your own beliefs and motivations, and align your mindset with your core beliefs, goals, and desires.

If you have set your sights on high achievement and high growth but wonder how you'll get there, then it's time to take a look at your own personal beliefs. If you wish you were more decisive, more at ease with delegating, taking risks, and embracing change, then you need to examine the underlying beliefs that guide your thoughts and actions.

It's time to take a vital first step toward developing your own high-achieving, turbo-growth mindset.

BELIEFS: YOUR OPERATING SYSTEM

The human brain is an amazing decision-making machine. By some estimates, your brain generates as many as 35,000 decisions every day.[1] Most of those decisions are trivial: I need to rub my nose. I want to change the radio station. I'll have another coffee.

Other daily decisions are more substantive: which role to recruit for next, which candidate best fits the role, which new products fit your value proposition, how to integrate new products into your offerings. Every action we take, every sentence we speak, requires rapid-fire choices at a rate of about 2,000 every waking hour, or one new choice every 1.8 seconds.[2]

We are capable of thinking and choosing so quickly because each of us operates from a set of unconscious fixed beliefs. These beliefs continuously feed our brain's scripted go-to criteria for making instantaneous choices, and the results of those choices reinforce our beliefs.

This unconscious feedback loop is your operating system. It functions silently in the background, just as your computer's operating system does. Our beliefs allow us to run our daily lives as though we've been programmed, with little awareness of the coding that limits our perceived range of options. Those limits help us think and act quickly, unconsciously, while also silently limiting our sense of possibilities. The value of thinking outside the box comes from looking at a situation free of preformed assumptions and fixed beliefs.

---

1. Joel Hoomans, "35,000 Decisions: The Great Choices of Strategic Leaders," *The Leading Edge*, blog, Roberts Wesleyan College, March 20, 2015, go.roberts.edu/leadingedge/the-great-choices-of-strategic-leaders; and Jamie Nicole LaBuzetta, and B. J. Sahakian, *Bad Moves: How Decision Making Goes Wrong*, and the Ethics of Smart Drugs (Oxford University Press, 2013).

2. Eva Krockow, "How Many Decisions Do We Make Each Day?" *Psychology Today*, September 27, 2018, www.psychologytoday.com/us/blog/stretching-theory/201809/how-many-decisions-do-we-make-each-day.

FIXED BELIEFS

Fixed beliefs set in our minds might include ideas such as:

- "I know better."

- "I'm special."

- "I need to be taken care of."

- "Everyone is an idiot."

- "You can't trust people."

Beliefs of this kind can appear in our minds as factual, as part of our reality, because we have relied on some of them since we were very young. If we didn't have fixed beliefs to sort and direct our thoughts and actions quickly, our brains might take ten minutes to run through all the possible answers to the question "How are you?"

Fixed beliefs are like lenses that determine how we see the world. Over time, we unconsciously believe that what we see through our fixed beliefs is a true representation of reality. That can be very destructive because our fixed beliefs don't give us the full picture. We tend to see and hear only the things that confirm the version of reality presented by those beliefs.

I once conducted an employee assessment of someone I'll call Richard. He was a key employee who was being considered for a leadership position within his firm. As I took Richard through the portion of the assessment that elicited his fixed beliefs, a very powerful fixed belief emerged: Richard believed that his coworkers were all idiots.

In his follow-up interview, Richard went on to share stories that detailed his frustrations in dealing with colleagues and subordinates at the firm. His description of each circumstance seemed aimed at justifying his fixed belief that all of them were idiots.

This was a big problem for Richard, and for his employer. His coworkers weren't idiots at all. Richard's attachment to his fixed belief about them was so strong, however, that he had little appreciation for when they did things right, or when he shared some of the blame when things went wrong. A fixed belief that does not change in the face of evidence to the contrary is the textbook definition of a delusion. Richard's conviction that his coworkers were idiots bordered on delusional thinking. That made him an unacceptable candidate for a leadership role at his firm.

YOUR SELF-LIMITING BELIEFS

And yet, there's something even more destructive than the fixed beliefs we harbor about others. It's the self-limiting beliefs we hold about ourselves. These are usually expressed as negative self-talk. It's that nagging inner voice that says you can't do something, and you shouldn't even try:

- "I'm not smart enough."

- "I'm no good at this."

- "I'm over the hill."

- "I'm not *fill in the blank* enough."

- "I'm not a *fill in the blank* kind of person."

In my experience, these self-limiting beliefs are the primary factor preventing most achievers from becoming high achievers. That voice inside has been with you since childhood. Psychologists call it the inner critic, and it's there as a survival adaptation. It protects you from physical harm, and it protects your ego from hurt and disappointment. The trouble is that it does so at the expense of your personal growth and self-expression. Your inner critic voices self-limiting beliefs that undermine your efforts to achieve the vision and goals you have today and discourage you from setting larger and more ambitious goals for the future.

Do high achievers experience negative self-talk? Of course they do. They're human. The difference with high achievers is that they don't *believe* that voice. They don't let these fleeting thoughts harden into self-limiting beliefs. They know that this inner critic is not a friend. In twelve-step programs, there is a wonderful acronym to define the meaning of FEAR: false evidence appearing real. That is what your inner critic is always telling you: a steady stream of false evidence appearing real.

YOUR CORE BELIEFS

Beyond these two sets of beliefs that commonly hold us back, there is a third set of beliefs that propels us forward. These are our core beliefs, our principles, the foundation blocks of who we are, who we want to be, how we think, how we behave, what we expect, and how we measure the world.

Core beliefs serve as our motivators. Ideally, they help us define the reasons—the *why*—behind everything we do, both in business and in our personal lives. They drive us forward and help us fight through hardship. In his classic bestseller *Man's Search for Meaning*, psychiatrist and Holocaust survivor Victor Frankl quoted Friedrich Nietzsche: "He who has a 'why' to live can bear almost any 'how.'"[3]

---

3. V. E. Frankl, *Man's Search for Meaning: An Introduction to Logotherapy* (New York: Simon & Schuster, 1984).

However, most people fail to live up to their core beliefs in the face of hardship and misfortune. Fixed beliefs and self-limiting beliefs pop up to protect us whenever the going gets tough. That's when they can do the greatest damage. If you're called upon to face a great challenge or to seize a great opportunity, you can't possibly prevail if you obey the inner voice that warns you that you're not up to the task. Through the lens of your fixed beliefs, your core beliefs may appear faulty or unrealistic when put to the test.

When you abandon faith in your core beliefs in these ways, your fixed beliefs and self-limiting beliefs can slowly eat away at your spirit. They can corrode and weaken your core beliefs, just as surely as rust over time can reduce a solid steel bar into dust.

Nonetheless, this is exactly how most people pass their days. We go through the motions of fulfilling the *what* and *how* of daily life. We do what is necessary to get by. Only high achievers truly live in their *why*: their core beliefs.

If you are an achievement-oriented entrepreneur, it's likely you've already overcome many of these obstacles to success intuitively. It's possible you hold some unconscious fixed beliefs that have been beneficial. A fixed belief that you are naturally superior to other people might have granted you the self-confidence to survive conditions where competitors have failed. Maybe you've developed a healthy habit of discounting negative self-talk. And it's possible that you hold other beneficial beliefs that you are not aware of. They are stored in your unconscious mind, functioning as hidden pathways for success.

To grow your business to the next level, though, you'll want to be present to all these hidden pathways, both the good and the bad. You want to understand them with your conscious mind. By raising your level of awareness level, you'll raise your results.

The price you pay is introspection. You must make the effort to examine your interior thoughts and unconscious motivations. The practice of introspection is how you can construct an accurate idea of who you really are. By employing introspection, you will focus your attention away from all of the external items distracting you from your core principles. Once you accept the premise that everything you accomplish in your life and through your business is rooted in your core beliefs, then you will recognize that the process of introspection is essential to becoming a high achiever.

THE VISION BOARD

Dave Mazzetti knew what he wanted. He hired us to coach him to the top. Dave wanted to rank in the top 1 percent at his firm in terms of productivity. He jokingly told me, "I'll do anything I need to do to become in the top 1 percent. If you tell me to stand outside my office with a sandwich board to bring on new clients, I'll do it."

One of the first steps in becoming a high achiever is to have a vision of what you want and where you want to go. We start by having you create a vision board of images that represent your dreams for yourself and your loved ones. This is an exercise that forces you to start thinking, perhaps for the first time ever, what you really value in life. The exercise also makes you recognize personal core values that you've been neglecting, at the expense of your spirit. By assembling a set of images to represent your desired future, you can begin to bring all of your core beliefs, fixed beliefs, and self-limiting beliefs out from your unconscious mind and into the open.

Dave knew he wanted to have financial control and a house on a lake, to be a great dad and a great husband, and to contribute to charity. His vision board represented all of these things. The images he presented, however, also revealed a thinking pattern we call outside in. Dave was driven by status, recognition, and other extrinsic motivations. He hired us to help him achieve the specific external goal of being among the top 1 percent at his firm. His vision board revealed as much. His goals were about outward appearance, recognition, and how others viewed him.

That is where Dave's thinking was at the time. As a lot of self-made businesspeople do, he owed much of his success to his youthful determination to make something of himself, to be somebody. His beliefs about what's important had developed over the years without much thought on Dave's part. In this respect, Dave is a typical entrepreneur when it comes to introspective thinking. Entrepreneurs are naturally action oriented, and not likely to sit and examine their thoughts and feelings very often.

But introspection leads to self-awareness: an understanding of the ways in which you are separate from your environment and from other people. That self-awareness gives you room to appreciate what makes you different, and how you can build your own unique set of principles, values, and beliefs from the inside out, from the person you really are.

For someone like Dave, who had achieved so much success through a certain set of fixed beliefs, it was very likely that those same beliefs would prevent him getting to the next level of success. Fixed beliefs are *fixed*. As such, they are likely to keep you fixed in one place unless you raise your awareness of them and actively work to unfix them. Introspection leads to awareness. Awareness leads to action. Action busts through fixed beliefs. By acting counter to fixed beliefs, the results drain those beliefs of their power.

Over the following three years we worked with Dave on improving his business results. At the same time, we took him through the process of defining his core values, but from the inside out: from what was important to him personally, regardless of what other people thought or said. This was a new perspective on life for Dave, and perfectly appropriate for a husband and father of four who was approaching middle age.

Two things happened in year four of our coaching with Dave Mazzetti. After three solid years of exceptional growth, Dave reached his goal of entering the top 1 percent. And when he did, it felt empty.

Dave, by then, had done enough introspective work on all his beliefs that this feeling of emptiness led him to a profound personal realization: money and recognition weren't part of his vision for his life after all. He also realized what he'd sacrificed in achieving his goal in the previous three years. He'd neglected his health. He was carrying more than 240 pounds on his five-foot-six frame. And he was neglecting his family, too. He'd bought the lake house of his dreams, which his family loved. But Dave was rarely there to enjoy it with them. He was always working.

When you question your core beliefs, you have to ask yourself: What do you stand for? What do you believe? What are your fundamentals? What are your tenets? What are your values? From there you can isolate the beliefs and philosophies most important in guiding your business, whether it's serving clients, serving team members, a sales philosophy, or a positioning philosophy. The list is potentially endless, so we usually ask clients to settle on just three main ideas as their points of focus. From there, they can examine those three core beliefs in terms of what changes in behaviors they would need to put them into action.

When your core beliefs produce new behaviors, those behaviors produce results that reflect and reinforce your core beliefs.

So Dave started to make a new vision board. It took him almost four months to finish. But his new board represented an inside-out version of his future, one in which *health* was the focus: physical health, financial health, emotional health, friendship, mentorship. As ever, Dave still wants to be a great father and husband, but he now operates from the inside out, with his inner values and beliefs driving his outward behaviors.

WHAT'S YOUR DASH?

The final page on Dave's vision board shows images of tombstones and graveyards, with the question "How am I filling my dash?" It's a reference to the dash following the birth date on the grave markers of living people. The date of death is still undetermined. How will you fill your remaining days to the right of that dash?[4]

Does that seem morbid? It may seem that way to some, but to me, it shows just how powerful the process of introspection can be. If you cannot deal with the essential awareness that your days are numbered, then you risk living in denial, unable to summon the courage to act on your core beliefs. Psychologists and philosophers writing on mortality hit this common note: your ability to be fully alive is largely determined by how you well you grasp the idea that one day you won't be.

Now, when Dave goes on his daily run (he's lost sixty pounds in three years), he keeps the final three images on his vision board in mind as the three areas of his life he wants to contemplate: his vision of his future, his giving up of old resentments and regrets, and lastly, his contributions to the world, how he plans to fill the rest of his days with meaning.

Dave now reaps the rewards of a new-found self-awareness, of his core beliefs, and of the relaxed grip his old, fixed beliefs and

---

4.   This concept is also described in poem by Linda Ellis called "The Dash," Copyright © 2020 Inspire Kindness, thedashpoem.com.

self-limiting beliefs had on him. Awareness of this kind is a rare thing when you're not consciously working on your core beliefs and values in this way. If you are like most entrepreneurs, you are buried deep in the trenches of your business. You don't make the time to create self-awareness about your business to see how deep you have dug and which way the tunnel is going.

Occasionally you might get a rude awakening, a moment of self-consciousness or embarrassment that brings you in touch with self-awareness, but that's rarely a positive or productive experience. Most of us usually snap right back into our programmed behaviors, with our unconscious beliefs running at full speed. It's a relief to have our conscious awareness reduced in that moment, which is how fixed beliefs and self-limiting beliefs sustain themselves, persist, and grow stronger in our unconscious minds.

But when you are actively engaged in an introspective process, when you use your vision board daily to raise your conscious awareness of your core values, you are more likely to make many of your 32,000 decisions that day based on the values that are most important to you. And the more self-aware you are, the more likely you are to engage in behavior that is true to who you are.

YOUR OWN ENTREPRENEURIAL MINDSET

In reading Dave's example, which of the values on his vision board resonate with you the most? Which of the four markers of high achievers get the most back-talk from your inner voice, from your self-limiting beliefs? Perhaps you've already identified a significant fixed belief that you know is out of whack with your values.

Only you can decide which beliefs matter most when it comes to what influences and motivates you. The coach in me would have you complete an assessment to determine those beliefs, with no hints or guidance from me. But you picked up this book to learn how to be a better entrepreneur, so let's set aside the normal coaching protocol.

Instead, I've provided four exercises in this chapter that walk you through the process of identifying your values, the elements of your vision board, your fixed beliefs, and your core beliefs. I strongly recommend you stop and write the answers for each step in each exercise. For your convenience, we have copies of these exercises and other exercises throughout the book available to download on the D2 website: dynamicdirections-d2.com/the3ceos.

It's tempting to keep reading all the way through, but to get the most value from the book, it's important to pause and follow the exercises. Writing out your own answers to these questions will raise your awareness of what's at stake for you in reading this book. It will enrich and personalize your experience of every chapter that follows.

EXERCISE 1.1
Your Beliefs

Below are forty beliefs that in my experience are commonly shared by entrepreneurs. I've altered the catchphrase of my favorite comedian Jeff Foxworthy ("You might be a redneck if . . . ") and presented this list in a similar format.

You might be an entrepreneur if you . . .

- believe in the art of the possible
- are addicted to change
- take risks
- manage risks
- set and exceed goals regularly
- are driven to the point of borderline obsession with your business affairs
- perform at the top of your field and/or industry
- embrace and love challenges
- find opportunities in challenges and adversity
- leap into the unknown
- are a lifetime learner
- hustle
- are an action taker
- are a results maker
- project a bullish attitude and see life through an optimistic lens
- say, "Yes, we can!" ninety times more than "No, we can't"
- are first in and last out at work each day

- are tenacious
- are passionate about what you believe and do
- tolerate uncertainty, can withstand the feeling of potential failure
- are a fear fighter (and win often!)
- are a visionary
- are self-confident, with a strong sense of self
- are flexible
- defy conventional wisdom to find solutions

- are rebellious (you break rules without jail time)
- prefer not to work for others
- are street savvy
- are flexible
- are a master at interpreting the value you offer with your businesses
- are a networker (connections and relationships are the name of the game)
- are patient but constructively dissatisfied

- are resilient
- are dedicated
- are a team player
- are system oriented
- understand that failure is a part of the game
- make use of ideas that arise from failed ventures
- are highly adaptable
- have strong money management skills
- know how to sell and promote
- practice meaningful work every minute of the day

Write down your answers to these three questions:

- Which ones matter *the most* to you?

- Which ones are not a part of you?

- Which ones are new for you?

Did I miss any beliefs that are important to you?

Add them to that list.

It's a good bet that everything in your business flows from the list of the beliefs you just wrote down. This is the set of beliefs that every day determines your behaviors. which produce your results, which reinforce your beliefs.

Now it's time to try doing your own vision board. My experience is that most of us tend to recoil from exercises like this one because it's a right-brain exercise that requires creativity, self-awareness, strategic thinking, and emotion. We're in a left-brain industry filled with analysis, statistics, and research reports. For most of us, scripting out a vision board takes us out of our comfort zone. But that's why it works so well. It opens our minds to possibilities unavailable to us if we stay in our left-brain thought patterns.

My own vision board is a simple PowerPoint presentation with images that help connect to what I value most, the life I want, and the person I want to become. Within the images are words and phrases that express the beliefs, personal values, and universal principles each image represents.

There are no explicit rules for doing a vision board. You must do it your way in order to gain a more authentic understanding of yourself and your purpose. But certain approaches have proven to be more effective than others. It's vital that you use the vision board to *dream*. You should represent dreams that will require enormous changes in your life, and a radical departure from how you live now. Your vision board should give you a feeling of its impossibility. That's what gives the vision board its power to inspire you.

EXERCISE 1.2
Your Vision Board

To get started on your vision board, answer these two questions:

- What is important to me that I am paying EXCELLENT attention to?

- What is important to me that I am NOT PAYING ENOUGH attention to?

Answering these questions truthfully will help you identify your values: the things that are really important to you in life. Consider things such as your family, career, physical environments, recreation, health, money, significant other, and more.

Keep your answers to one or two words. Once you have these lists, find or create images that represent these values and put them on your vision board.

This might be a physical piece of paper, or it might be a computer screen—whatever works best for you.

This exercise is also available to download from our website: dynamicdirections-d2.com/the3ceos.

Many of the items you include on your vision board will cost money, but it's important to avoid the temptation of assigning dollar costs to the images. Your values, not your bank account balance, will drive you forward as you confront the fears, obstacles, and uncertainties that always accompany big changes.

Once you have constructed your vision board, you must keep it alive so you can stay focused on the values you are striving for. Put your vision board in a place where you can see it often. Make it a point to study it for sixty seconds every morning so you can envision yourself living out your vision board values throughout your day. Share it with family, friends, and significant people in your life who can help you attain the life and business you have outlined on your board.

Nothing will propel you forward faster than creating a clear vision of where you want to go.

REFRAME, RETHINK, REFOCUS

Now let's dig in. Time to raise your self-awareness and get some ROI from all this introspection. Try to list three self-limiting beliefs that you think are holding you back. Use all the tools we've just gone over to help identify them.

What does your inner critic tell you in times of stress, when sticking to your core values is most at risk? "I can't do this." "I'm too old for this." "I've done enough already."

What's the FEAR (false evidence appearing real) that the inner critic serves up when your courage is put to the test? That's one of your self-limiting beliefs. The voice is a siren song of defeat. It's an opinion. It's not the truth. High achievers probably hear the voice just as loudly as you do. They just don't obey.

"I've got to be perfect."

"I can't afford it."

"This always happens to me."

"This is for people richer than me."

"I can't trust anyone."

EXERCISE 1.3
Your Fixed Beliefs

- Write down three fixed beliefs that you suspect are preventing you from experiencing what we call the art of the possible.

- Where are your fixed beliefs standing between you and high achievement?

When you write down these beliefs, their grip on you relaxes. They are powerful forces in your unconscious mind, but out in the open, they appear as they are: just thoughts. These are assertions based on obsolete or distorted information. They are meant to protect you, to keep you playing small and safe.

Is that what you want running your life? Running your business? Of course not.

Even those beliefs that might seem beneficial and success oriented (such as believing you know best, or that you must work harder than everyone else) should be examined for their downsides. What happens when you experience something that shakes your fixed belief?

Perhaps you encounter people who seem to know more than you do, or who achieve success without working quite so hard. Do you embrace them and ask their advice? That's unlikely if they're threatening one of your fixed beliefs. Instead, you feel threatened. You get angry. You look for their faults. You grow bitter about an unfair world.

If you can get all these beliefs defined and out in the open, you are on your way to thinking, acting, and achieving what you want. But don't underestimate the power of these beliefs, because it only takes one fixed belief, that hidden pathway in your mind, to put you on a course of failing to live up to your vision of your future. Never forget that your fixed beliefs are dangerous because they always put you at risk of destructive, delusional thinking.

You can't deny or wish away your self-limiting and fixed beliefs. They are as much a part of you as your hand or foot. But with introspection, you have the chance to reframe, rethink, and refocus these beliefs so they generate productive behaviors in your business. If you can interpret your vision of the future into a series of business beliefs, you can begin to align those beliefs with the behaviors that will generate the results you want.

The list of beliefs for every business is unique. Such core values statements commonly address these themes:

- serving clients

- serving team members

- marketing services and products

- sales philosophy

- positioning philosophy

- operations

- core products and services (at least three)

EXERCISE 1.4
Your Core Beliefs

- List the three strong beliefs that guide your business.

- Ask yourself what beliefs you'd want all your employees to express every day.

- Ask yourself which of your personal beliefs you'd want to be transmitted through your employees to your clients and other stakeholders in the business.

As you complete this exercise, you will see and feel your introspection ROI begin to climb. The more self-aware you become, the more clearly you can see your beliefs expressed through your business, the behaviors of you and your employees aligned with those beliefs, and the results reinforcing the behaviors.

BELIEFS AND BEHAVIORS IN ACTION

After defining your list of beliefs, write out a list of desired results you want from your business. These are the specific, defined results you want in the short term. You can think big, but for this exercise you want to keep the desired results measurable in the short term.

Now for each desired result, write out one of your positive beliefs and one of your negative beliefs associated with that result. For example, if your desired result is five new clients this month, you might write your positive belief that your business offers unique benefits to new clients. A negative belief, fixed or self-limiting, might be that this month is a bad time to gain five new clients or your firm doesn't have the infrastructure to support this growth.

Now write the positive and negative behaviors you associate with each belief—basically, what happens when you act on your core beliefs, and what happens when you act on your fixed and self-limiting beliefs.

Again, those fixed and self-limiting beliefs aren't going anywhere. The question is how you align your behaviors. Do you align them with the core beliefs you've consciously embraced in adulthood, or with those fixed and self-limiting beliefs you've been unconsciously nurturing since you were a child?

When doing this final exercise, give some thought to framing your desired business results along the lines of those four markers for high achievers:

1. High achievers implement change at a rapid pace.

2. High achievers excel at managing risk.

3. High achievers leverage their resources.

4. High achievers are decisive.

First, define a desired business result corresponding to each of these behaviors.

Then, take each result through the same positive/negative belief/behavior exercise just described.

Now look at what you've written. It's likely that you have brought out from your unconscious mind the exact set of fixed and self-limiting beliefs—and resulting negative behaviors—that are your personal obstacles to high achievement.

These are the unconscious beliefs you've been fulfilling when your performance falls short in these four critical areas. You can see the negative behaviors you're prone to indulge, and the positive behaviors that your core beliefs would have you embrace.

It was out of an exercise like this that one of our clients—I'll call her Pamela—recognized that her financial planning advice was worth far more than she had been charging. Dispensing wise advice came so easily and naturally to her that she had developed an unconscious belief it wasn't worth very much.

Once Pamela recognized the disconnect between the great value she was creating and her small, one-time fees, she began charging higher monthly fees for ongoing advice. This was difficult for her because she also had to overcome her concern that she might not be able to deliver advice reliably on an ongoing basis.

It took some work to develop a menu of services that articulated the value she offered in a way that her clients would understand. Pamela greatly increased her engagements and grew her business as a result. But the essential first step was doing an exercise that revealed how undervaluing her advice was a fixed belief that had trapped her into playing small.

This exercise is not easy to do. For many, the results may be hard to look at. Congratulations for completing it. Remember that the vast majority of people go through their entire lives without ever achieving this level of self-awareness. You've gone where most other people fear to tread because you are committed to being a high achiever.

You should refer to these insights about yourself on a daily basis. The stakes will keep rising, and so will the challenges, so the daily work of reframing, rethinking, and refocusing your beliefs is never done.

Then redo this process periodically, as you grow and establish new self-reinforcing patterns of belief leading to behaviors, behaviors leading to results, and results informing your beliefs.

The Turbo-Growth Mindset

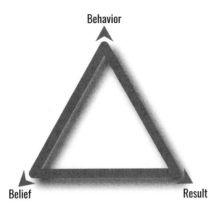

We call this virtuous cycle the alignment triangle. In architecture and engineering, there is no stronger, more stable structure than the triangle, because the three angles of a triangle are fixed and immobile.

That's how it is with your beliefs, your behaviors, and your results. The relationship of all three to each other is rock solid, predictable, and dependable. Change your beliefs, and your behaviors will shift. Change your behaviors and your results will improve. Then learn from your results to inform your beliefs. Use the driving force of your core beliefs to bring all three into an alignment triangle, and it will become the sturdy foundation on which you will build all your future success.

TURBO GROWTH
Three Questions

The Mindset
What do you think is your biggest obstacle to achieving turbo growth?

The Practice
Which of your fixed beliefs can you try reframing today?

The Opportunity
What's the vision that gets you out of bed each day and makes you want to pursue it with the fire of a thousand suns?

CHAPTER TWO

Intentional Congruence

Lester Matlock had become so successful that his commitments were getting the best of him. Along with his growing financial planning firm in Little Rock, Arkansas, Lester ran a prosperous real estate development company with nine properties and three projects under construction. Over the years, as Lester raised his profile, he added a series of civic and philanthropic boards to his plate and served on almost a dozen of them.

As Lester's calendar grew more crowded and his days grew longer and longer, he would often come home in the evenings feeling drained. For all the energy he was expending, he had no real sense he was making progress anywhere. "My mom used to say you can tire yourself out running in place and not getting anywhere," Lester said. "When those kinds of thoughts bubble up, I know it can lead to fatigue and burnout."

He wasn't sure how to address the situation until he attended one of our firm's workshops on entrepreneurial fundamentals. During an exercise on intentional congruence, a term and concept developed by Dr. Qubein, Lester began to see his situation in a new light.

As Dr. Qubein describes it, intentional congruence is a method of decision making in which you choose activities that are aligned with your larger goals and vision, and you reject ones that aren't. Ideally, intentionally congruent activities are also aligned with each other in ways that are mutually supportive.

The process revealed to Lester that many of his obligations failed the test. He didn't enjoy managing his real estate properties, and with three new development projects coming up, that workload was due to get heavier. When he looked at his list of board memberships, he recognized that his heart wasn't in many of them. They were becoming burdensome obligations.

"I was involved in a lot of stuff, and I questioned, 'Where am I going and what am I doing?'" he recalled. Through this intentional congruence exercise, he began to identify for the first time where his passions were, which activities were congruent with those passions, and which activities "were things that I just kind of said yes to, but my heart wasn't in it."

Every one of us has limited amounts of time, attention, and energy to invest in ourselves, accomplish our goals, and build our businesses. And yet, because of our success, we tend to accumulate commitments that take a toll on us. We say yes to various opportunities and commitments because we can, but we tend to underestimate their cumulative impact on our sense of well-being and balance in our lives.

"I woke up after going through that exercise," Lester said. "I realized I couldn't do all these things. I couldn't be all these things." The first thing to go was his real estate business. He remembered being at a ballgame on a rare night out when he got a text from one of his tenants: a video of water running down from a second-floor burst pipe. His evening's enjoyment was done as he spent the rest of the game trying to track down his out-of-state contractor at 10 p.m. He decided he didn't want that responsibility; it wasn't necessary.

Intentional Congruence

"I said, 'I'm done,'" he recalled. "This isn't bringing life to me." He called up his real estate agent and instructed him to put all nine real estate properties on the market. Then he cancelled the four or five construction projects that were either planned or already underway. Next, he resigned from two of his boards and notified two others that he would be leaving later that year when his term was up.

That's the first stage of intentional congruence: sorting out what doesn't fit in your future. In going through the process, you write down your various areas of activity and score each one for how connected it is to your other areas, the size of the potential financial rewards, and your readiness to execute a change.

Besides exposing areas that are isolated drains on your time and energy, this exercise can force fresh thinking on the possibilities for synergies among what you may have assumed were disconnected activities. That's the second stage: discovering ways to maximize your results through synergy, leverage, and interlocking opportunities.

Think of the efficiency you achieve when you buy twenty items in one supermarket visit instead of going to the supermarket twenty times. By combining all your purchases in a single trip, the cost of traveling to the store and back is amortized over all twenty items, reducing the effective expense of each item and saving you a significant amount of time.

It's no different with intentional congruence. Daily life constantly prompts you to focus on each of your activities separately, the equivalent of making separate trips to the supermarket. This exercise offers you the chance to consider where there is congruence among your activities, and where there are opportunities to move forward on two or three of those activities at the same time—to keep them in the family, so to speak.

The resulting insights can lead to unexpected and astonishing results. My wife and I own a boutique art gallery and gift store called

Studio Slant, but until I included it in the intentional congruence exercise, I'd never considered the possible synergies between the store and my other business interests. In my coaching for entrepreneurs, I have long stressed the value of showing gratitude to your clients by giving gifts that amaze and delight them. Then it finally dawned on me that with the help of Studio Slant, I could provide my coaching clients with much better and more specific advice in this regard. For years, I'd overlooked this way of literally keeping it in the family. I had been wasting opportunities to serve my clients and benefit Studio Slant at the same time.

We now send our clients a curated quarterly gift guide that showcases gift ideas from Studio Slant and other gift stores as well. My wife regularly attends our workshops to meet our clients and participates in our programs about enhancing the client experience. We eventually added the building that houses Studio Slant to our portfolio of real estate holdings, with intentional congruence in mind.

The very idea of turbo growth is based on the design of the superefficient turbocharged engine, a prime example of synergistic intentional congruence. A turbocharged engine harnesses energy from exhaust gases—wasted energy in most engines—to drive a compressor that forces more air into the cylinders. That enables the engine to produce more power from the same amount of fuel. What could be a more perfect image of intentional congruence and turbo growth?

EXERCISE 2.1
Your Intentional Congruence Map

Take a moment now to draw a circle in the middle of a sheet of paper and write your name in it. Then draw more circles around the center circle and write inside each circle the area of your life that it represents: your family, your business, your community involvement, another business you own, the youth sports team you coach, hobbies, interests, and so on.

As you're writing down your categories, focus on the areas that drive your passion and productivity. When you're at your highest levels of passion and productivity, your satisfaction level is typically pretty high. Now, draw lines of connection among them. In my case, for instance, I'd draw lines between Studio Slant, my commercial real estate firm, and my coaching practice.

- First assess them for alignment.
  - Which ones are aligned with your purpose?
  - Which ones aren't?

- Then assess them on the basis of fulfillment.
  - Which ones create the most fulfillment for you?
  - Which ones create the least?

- Now look for connections.
  - What are the strongest connections and how can you make them stronger?
  - What is most connected to everything else? Why?
  - What is least connected, and what will you do about it?

- Finally, look at balance.
  - What is your balance point right now?
  - Where are you off-balance?
  - How will you adjust?

This exercise is also available to download from our website: dynamicdirections-d2.com/the3ceos.

The idea behind this exercise is to connect as many of the circles as possible. The more circles that connect to each other, the more benefit you're getting from your investment of time and energy. With connected circles, you're getting more return on investment with less energy expended. Where no lines exist, ask yourself how the circles might be better connected. Look at your strong lines of connection and ask yourself how you might replicate that kind of synergy.

In Lester's case, he realized that managing real estate was not fulfilling for him. He didn't enjoy it and decided to sell his holdings. But he still wanted to maintain a significant investment in real estate that was aligned with his financial goals and his purpose.

The insight prompted him to look for connections. He viewed his real estate investment possibilities through the lens of his marketing activities. How could he invest the proceeds from his real estate sales in a way that connected with his client base?

Once Lester knew what he wanted, it didn't take long for him to find it. One of his clients introduced him to a major real estate developer, who invited Lester to join his small group of seventeen private investors.

As the eighteenth silent partner in this investment group, Lester saw new opportunities for intentional congruence. He wanted his new partners as clients. For the holidays, Lester invited his seventeen new partners to a party at his house. The enjoyable hours he spent decorating and preparing the house for the party were hours he never had to spare in the years when he was managing real estate properties.

"In choosing to get rid of some stuff in my life," Lester said, "it's actually opening up doors for other things."

Next, Lester turned to one of the passions in his life: boxing and mixed martial arts. For years, Lester had been involved in these sports in gyms all over the Little Rock area. He knew all the gym owners very well. Now, for the very first time, he found himself asking why, among all the gym owners he knew so well, he had never invited any of them to be his clients.

So he hosted a dinner for them to acknowledge their significance in his life and to thank them. Next, he thought of his wife's favorite jewelry shop. Why not host an event there for his top-tier clients, and also for the spouses of his seventeen new real estate partners?

"I'm seeing it everywhere I go," Lester said of intentional congruence. "How do I connect all the things that I want to put time into, the things I have the most interest in, the most passion?"

IT STARTS WITH SAYING NO

When you begin working on the intentional congruence exercise, you may find that the first, most painful price you pay is the need to start saying no more often.

When Lester Matlock decided to drop his board commitments, he knew he would leave some people feeling disappointed. And canceling the real estate developments he'd planned was unhappy news for his building contractor, who had been counting on those projects for a large portion of his 2019 revenue.

A reluctance to say no is how Lester got so overcommitted in the first place. That's true for most of us. Saying no is often unpleasant, which is a reason why we so often default to being agreeable and going along with things we don't really want.

The intentional congruence exercise makes it easy to say no because for the first time ever, you're living in your *why*. You have criteria for saying yes or no to choices presented to you. Once you have a high level of clarity about what you want in your business and your life, it's much simpler to recognize what you don't want.

"I've adopted a mentality that if I don't absolutely love it, I don't buy it," Lester said. "If it's not something that strikes my heart immediately, I say no to it. It was a tough thing to recognize that 'No,' in and of itself, is truly a complete sentence."

The clarity of intentional congruence makes it much easier to say no with grace and without hard feelings. When you limit your commitments to those activities that line up with the other interests important in your life, any opportunity to go outside those commitments shows up as a poor investment of time, energy, and dollars.

For example, if people ask you to make a donation to their favorite charity, you might explain that while you admire their cause and wish them well, unfortunately all your charitable resources are committed elsewhere. Most people will appreciate your honesty.

Saying no is a learnable skill, and for anyone who wants to achieve turbo growth, it is an essential competency. It's self-evident that as you grow faster and raise your revenues, you will also see an exponential rise in business offers and opportunities. If you don't have a process for dealing with all these pitches and bright ideas, they will back up in your mind (and on your desk). Your forward momentum will suffer.

Greg McKeown, author of *Essentialism*[5], has a simple two-step process for evaluating opportunities requiring a fast yes/no answer. The first step, he suggests, is to establish in advance the three most important criteria that are your *absolute minimum* criteria for even considering the opportunity. The point is to say no quickly to opportunities that are not even worth exploring because they are not a fit with your goals. By setting your three minimum criteria right up front, you avoid being tempted to proceed on vague ballpark estimates of a desirable outcome, and then get yourself in trouble by compromising the number downward for fear of losing the deal.

---

5. Greg McKeown, *Essentialism: The Disciplined Pursuit of Less*. (New York: Crown Business, 2014).

Intentional Congruence

Say a friend wants you to join a real estate venture with him. Your minimum criteria for such a deal might be 1) commercial real estate only; 2) minimum investment of $500,000 to make it worth your while; and 3) your partner has to be capable of doing all planning and construction. If the proposed venture fails even one of these three minimum criteria, you can say no very quickly and definitively.

On the other hand, if the proposal meets or exceeds your three minimum criteria, you can put it to McKeown's second test: your ideal criteria. Does this opportunity promise enough upside to be worth risking your investment of time, attention, and money? Your ideal criteria might be 1) the property should produce a positive cash flow within thirty-six months, and 2) rental income should yield a return of at least eight percent over seven to twelve years.

Let's say the proposal is close to meeting your ideal criteria, but not quite. Your ideal criteria can serve as clear goals for negotiating terms that are more aligned with your expectations, while you retain the option of walking away if your ideal criteria aren't met. And if the proposed partnership passes all the tests for minimum and ideal criteria right off the bat—which is, admittedly, rare—you can proceed with the knowledge that you're moving ahead in alignment with your goals. At each stage of the decision-making process, you can rely on your minimum and ideal criteria as the numbers you must meet before proceeding to the next stage.

When it comes to buying another practice, there is one minimum criterion that rules all others: cultural fit. You should run away from any practice that doesn't share your core values, philosophies, and principles, no matter how appealing it might appear in terms of revenue. This is the one central principle I always pound home whenever I discuss practice acquisitions with potential buyers: "Don't chase money; chase culture!"

Assuming you find a practice that meets your minimum criteria for cultural fit, you then can establish other minimum criteria related to the seller's client base. The seller must have enough clients who would fit your firm's ideal client criteria to make a purchase worthwhile, although you can stretch your definition to include clients in the seller's client base who *could become* ideal clients with time and attention. What you don't want is to purchase a batch of clients whom you know you will need to sell to another practice because those clients will never fit your ideal criteria definition.

The other minimum criterion is talent. Even if the seller is a cultural fit with an attractive client base, it's not a good prospect if you lack the available talent to step in and run the new acquisition if the current owner retires or is incapacitated. If you double your client capacity but don't have additional advisors on your team to handle the meeting load, how will you handle the risk of leaving your clients poorly served? A subset of talent is your infrastructure and information systems. Do you have the capacity to create scale in your business to support the extra volume, or will growth saddle all your clients with a degradation in service?

You shouldn't bother looking at a potential practice purchase if it fails to meet any one of these three minimum criteria. Two out of three isn't good enough. Only when the deal fits all three is it worth your while to dig into the details of the practice's offerings and all the specifics about the client base, its investible assets, and prospects for growth. The acquisition process can be a long hard journey, so don't waste your time starting down that road if any of these three minimum criteria are lacking.

THE PAIN OF MISSED OPPORTUNITIES

There is an obvious trade-off in this approach. Sometimes you will find yourself declining what seems like a very good option because it doesn't quite fit the ideal criteria. To do that takes emotional maturity and a high level of emotional intelligence. To avoid buying for the sake of buying, you must have faith that the ideal option will come along soon enough.

The world is filled with missed opportunities. A dozen publishers passed on the first novel in the Harry Potter literary series that is worth $25 billion today. Every NFL team in the 2000 amateur draft skipped over a young quarterback named Tom Brady several times until he was finally selected in the sixth round as that year's 199th pick. A lot of smart investors passed on Amazon's IPO in 1997, when five shares were worth less than $100. Those same five shares were worth $120,000 twenty years later.

The costs of *not* saying no are not nearly as clear cut. The price paid by being indecisive or by saying yes far too often is much more insidious. It accumulates over time. It points to a more general problem with decision making.

We make decisions emotionally, but we prefer to think that our choices are rational, so we can lie to ourselves about how the decision was made. We rationalize, making the emotional choice first, and then very quickly identify a rational pretense for the choice. You tell yourself and friends why an expensive purchase makes sense, when the purchase was actually made on impulse because you wanted it.

This may seem like a harmless quirk on its surface, but psychologists who have studied rationalization say it can have a detrimental effect on your ability to learn from experience. If you're accustomed to telling yourself pleasant fibs about where your choices come from, you're subtly conditioning your mind to not face reality, and to not learn from experience. When you casually rationalize and diminish the reason for a recent setback, or why something went wrong, you may be missing the chance to learn an important lesson or important information about what really happened.

The simplest test of whether you're rationalizing is to consider the evidence supporting the opposite choice. Weighing both sides fairly in that way is essential to critical thinking. If you've worked on your self-awareness and recognized the tendencies of your fixed beliefs, you're more likely to catch yourself rationalizing.

A common pattern found among entrepreneurs is to be quick to decide, and then slow to change your mind once committed. In these cases, we see not only rationalization but the phenomenon called escalation of commitment, also known as throwing good money after bad.

High achievers don't make this kind of mistake nearly so often. They know who they are, where they're going, and how they want to get there. This clarity allows them to make decisions very quickly, including decisions to cut bait, and not escalate commitment to a previous decision that's proven to be a mistake.

EXERCISE 2.2
Your Daily Decision Making

- What decisions do you make on a daily and weekly basis?

- What kinds of decisions? How many?

- Which decisions do you find easy to make and which ones are difficult?

- List the kinds of decisions you find most difficult.

As you raise your awareness and confront the decisions that give you the most trouble, you can begin to make inroads that will help you avoid making emotional decisions and rationalizations that keep you tied to those decisions. All these decision processes are designed to drain decisions of their emotional content so you can make your own choices by design, not by default.

DELEGATING AND RISK

Entrepreneurs often have trouble delegating tasks, responsibilities, and decisions to others.

The eagerness to delegate is one of the clear markers of a high achiever, and micromanagement, by contrast, is a marker of those who achieve far below their abilities. If you're having trouble delegating, you may be a control freak.

If you're still keeping your own calendar or booking your own flights, it's time to take a hard look at what simple tasks you no longer need to hang on to. But that's just for starters. Delegation involves a much more important issue: leaders who delegate only minor or unimportant duties to team members are not really leading. Turbo growth isn't possible until you trust your team members to make their own decisions, and their own mistakes as well. There's a right way and a wrong way to do this, which I'll address in the next chapter, "Earning, Learning, and Serving."

One way to free up your time is to deliberately compress your decision making into a concentrated timeline, make the decision, and then move forward. This is a discipline that forces you to surrender further decision making to your team and frees you up to explore other, larger issues. Another form of this compression is to deliberately make a lot of decisions over a short period of time.

For example, I coach clients to avoid open-loop syndrome, where you are constantly expending mental energy because you have several decisions to make at the same time and you are letting the process drag out.

Write down all your pending decisions, make a choice and then move on. You should touch each decision only one time. If you just say you'll come back to it later, you will expend too much energy and waste too much time.

Another strategy is to have a regular, set time when you make decisions for your business. This way, you can move through all your decisions at once instead of constantly interrupting other work to deal with the latest question.

Ultimately, your reluctance to delegate suggests you might be too uncomfortable with risk, and there are no rewards that are risk-free. If you could take the risk out of life, you'd take all the opportunity out of life, as well. Risk is not something to be avoided; it's something to be managed.

To manage risk when deciding whether to pursue an opportunity, it's best to start by breaking down the possible outcomes in terms of impact:

- What is the best-case scenario as a result of your decision?

- What is the most likely case scenario?

- What is the worst-case scenario?

The common mistake is to consider these issues only in financial terms. Financial terms are usually the most important factor, but they're only one of several important factors.

Use this checklist to fully explore the risk-reward possibilities in these seven distinct categories:

☐ **Financial.** How much of your funds will this require? How much capital are you willing to risk? What's the potential ROI?

☐ **Reputational.** Will this enhance your reputation? What could go wrong? Does it matter?

☐ **Health.** Will you be out of balance?

☐ **Energy.** Will you have the energy for it, or will it drain you?

☐ **Relational.** Is there an opportunity to build new relationships or enhance established ones?

☐ **Emotional.** Based on your emotional competence, can you handle the potential stress of change?

☐ **Spiritual.** Does this fit with who I am?

Is it hard to pass up a financially promising deal because of these softer nonfinancial factors? Yes, but it's not as hard as you might think. I once coached a client who turned down two very lucrative merger offers purely due to his very real concerns about cultural fit. In using these principles, he put the financial considerations last because he trusted that the right cultural fit would come around eventually. And it did. The third merger opportunity proved to be the charm.

When you look at any prospective deal, it's important to see it through the lens of its opportunity cost. If that client had merged his firm with the first one that came along, he'd be miserable today. No amount of money could compensate him for the endless cultural issues he'd be dealing with. And at the same time, he'd never know what he'd missed by not waiting for a more culturally suitable merger partner to come along.

You should always plan for the worst and work for the best. If the worst case is something you can't live with, then the risk is not worth taking. Tufts University Professor Amar V. Bhide has done extensive studies of risk taking among entrepreneurs. He's found that the best entrepreneurs don't conform to the stereotypical image of what he calls the "irrational, overconfident risk seeker." Instead, the best entrepreneurs always try to minimize their downside risk before closing on deals, an approach Bhide frames as "Heads I win; tails I don't lose too much."

RISK AND CHANGE

The official motto of the US Marine Corps is *Semper fidelis* (always faithful). Its unofficial motto is a three-word operating imperative: improvise, adapt, and overcome.

What's true for the marines is true for everyone. How you anticipate change and how you react to change is how you manage risk and how you succeed.

Change is inevitable and there are four constant forces of change you should always keep an eye on in terms of risk to your firm.

1. **Market disruption.** What's your plan for when the market turns south? Do you know how to turn market disruption to your advantage after a shakeout of weaker competitors?

2. **Client erosion.** If your normal rate of client turnover were to accelerate, how long would it take for you to notice and take action? What trends are going on in your business that you need to address? What patterns are emerging that you haven't addressed?

3. **Considered consumption.** Your clients' needs may be changing, and competitors may be raising their expectations for service. What are you doing to reduce the risk of losing out when your clients' needs and buying habits change?

4. **Opportunity correction.** How do you plan to reduce the impact of losses when something goes wrong? Do you have the resources in place so that a mistake with a major client is recoverable and won't lead to loss of the client? Reacting in a timely manner and showing that you're sorry can actually strengthen a relationship, but only if you're prepared to do this when the mistake is made.

THE RISKS OF NOT CHANGING

You may go some time with none of these business risks substantially affecting you. If that's the case, you may be susceptible to complacency: the risk of not changing with the times until it's too late.

In tennis, they say you should never change a winning game, but the rules of tennis never change, while business rules in every industry are being disrupted all the time. High achievers know they must change even their most successful programs and projects to stay ahead of the curve and not fall victim to these four risks:

1. **Lost talent.** Never forget that high-achieving employees want to be with winners. Many of my clients have poached top talent from other practices that weren't as dynamic and growth oriented.

2. **Lost clients.** What's your retention rate? Repeat business rate? Where might your clients go to get another product

or service that you don't offer? You must constantly monitor your value interpretation with clients, or they will conclude you're not hearing their needs. And they will be right.

3. **Lost relevance.** When your firm and its services begin to lose relevance in the marketplace, your first two risks may intensify. You begin to lose talent and clients. Make sure you continue to invest in your personal knowledge of changes in the field and extend those investments to your employees.

4. **Lost credibility.** How well are you regarded by peers and colleagues you rely on for referrals? There is always a risk, as a new generation rises, for some longtime players to get crowded out, no longer viewed deserving of running in the same circle. The result can be a rapid decline of opportunities, putting the firm in a downward spiral because opportunities to grow and change become limited with loss of credibility.

These last two points in particular indicate the ultimate method of risk management, which is to invest in your support systems. Coaching, mastermind groups, advisory boards, industry groups—involvement in all of them will tend to keep you mindful and on high alert for the imperative to change.

One of our clients, Jay Woerdeman, has taken this warning totally to heart. He's driven by the idea that "If I don't evolve, I'll lose. I'll go extinct." He's constantly leading his team forward, asking, "Where are we going and how are we going to get there?" He recognizes the danger of complacency, as few other people I know do, because he understands the very real risk of gradually losing relevance in our fast-changing industry and one day becoming a dinosaur.

SUCCESS REDEFINED

For Lester Matlock, success has been redefined in the years since he first did the intentional congruence exercise. "I'm not impressed with the people who tell me they're so busy they don't have time for anything," he said. "I've found that the most successful people are the ones who actually have time."

The time he's won back from being overextended has allowed him to work more closely on his financial advisor business and its offerings. He's taken six of his clients through the intentional congruence exercise. "With three of them, we were both in tears during the meeting because they realized how dissatisfied they were," he said. "These are successful folks, and they were running themselves ragged."

He also used intentional congruence to help his employees manage their work and career plans. In one case, the process helped him find a better role for a young woman in the company. In another case, it revealed one young employee's complete lack of passion for the field. "I could tell he was not happy," Lester said. He gave the young man some career books to read, helped him get his resume together, and coached him as he figured out his next steps toward exiting the company.

As he's achieved a sense of balance in his work life, that ethos has extended all the way into his wardrobe. One day he counted forty-six suits and twenty-six sport coats in his closet. Of the forty-six suits, he was only wearing about fifteen of them regularly, so he culled the other thirty. He donated them all to an organization that provides business attire for moderate-income employees who have a hard time affording such clothes.

Every year, Lester takes the company offsite for a retreat to discuss goals for the coming year. All team members present their goals and address how they will help each other meet those goals.

The theme of the most recent year was to be efficient, be effective, be intentional.

A lot of time was spent on intentional congruence. What began as Lester Matlock's personal issue with his real estate and board obligations has ended up benefiting his business and all its employees. It's made him a better, more effective leader, a true chief executive officer.

"What it's allowed me to do is recenter and refocus," he said. "I'm spending the majority of my time doing the stuff I want to do. And that's something that I can't really put a price on."

INTENTIONAL CONGRUENCE
Three Questions
The Mindset
If you stopped your least enjoyable activity,
what would you do with your extra time and energy?

The Practice
Where do you need the most practice saying no?

The Opportunity
How can you align more of your activities and roles
to maximize your time, talent, and resources?

CHAPTER THREE

Earning, Learning, and Serving

As are all the people I coach, Dave Mazzetti and Lester Matlock were both extremely successful business leaders when we began our work together. By nearly all measures, they had entered mid-life having exceeded many of their own expectations for themselves. What opened up for them next, perhaps something they had never anticipated, was an expansion of their notion of success, to one of significance.

We can define success as the achievement of personal goals and accomplishments rewarded with measurable material triumphs: houses, cars, and all the other things money can buy.

The difference between success and significance, as my mentor, Dr. Nido Qubein, has taught me, is that your success can be admired from afar, while your significance is felt in people's hearts.

Success is materialistic. Significance is spiritual. Success is money-based, goal-oriented, and self-serving. Significance is mission-based, purpose-oriented, and serves others. Success is all about fans, fame, and fortune. Significance is all about faith, family, and friends.

Your turbo-growth mindset puts you on a journey from success to significance. Success is just one station on the journey, although it's a station many never travel beyond. If you want to lead a life full of purpose, one that makes a positive lasting impact on others, you can't afford to get stuck at success. In that sense, you might see success as an excellent direction, but a poor destination. That's because success only feeds your material desires. It will never feed your sense of fulfillment.

For an entrepreneur, success is the critical pathway to significance. Success sets the stage. It creates possibilities. It opens opportunities. Achieving success in the various facets of your life creates a natural magnetism to which people are drawn. Because of your success, people are likely to look to you for leadership and inspiration.

Success presents you with a number of big questions. How do you share your success? How do you pass along your gifts and knowledge so others can learn and grow with you? And how do you do this in ways that benefit your own personal growth and the growth of your business? How can you do this in a way that will live on long after your life is over?

TRANSFORMATIONAL LEADERSHIP

I never work with start-up businesses for a number of reasons, but the main one is that start-ups are striving for success, while my coaching operates in the realm beyond success. Every start-up struggles for survival, which calls mostly for a leadership style I would call transactional leadership. Raising revenue and reducing expenses are the prime objectives. Employees are assessed for their value against cost. Sales prospects are judged for their dollar-value potential, or perhaps their links to other big-dollar prospects.

This intense focus on sales makes sense in a start-up, or in any struggling business, for that matter. Everything must be seen in dollars and cents because any failure to grow revenue and control costs could sink the ship.

The leaders I work with have long passed this struggle phase and have reached an initial inflection point of success, achieved largely through transactional leadership. These leaders have soldiered through several steep learning curves. They've achieved a degree of stability and sustainability. At that point, leaders of such companies stand at a crossroads. Do they want to stay small and develop a boutique shop? Or do they want to continue to grow by addition and leverage?

There are trade-offs in either choice. To stay small by choice means you need to run a very disciplined boutique shop driven by niche marketing. You must carefully segment your clientele and very likely need to sell off or drop clients every eighteen months, just to avoid outgrowing your company's infrastructure. Maintaining a boutique practice of this kind can be very rewarding, but it takes constant diligence and reinvestment in your systems and your people to meet client expectations.

More often, I see business owners preferring to stay small just to avoid the headaches of growing larger. This is a nonstrategy that almost always ends in disaster. The company may sustain itself on the same big clients year after year, but when those clients change direction or die off, the firm's focus starts circling the drain because its biggest clients are disappearing. Outwardly the company and its owner may seem fine, but their unwillingness to invest in their business and marketing to bring on new clients is eroding their relevance a little bit every day. The disaster happens when the business owner doesn't even recognize the business is becoming less and less relevant.

In today's business environment, I believe that every company that is not growing is dying. Nonetheless, many entrepreneurs would rather remain small with no formal growth plans than risk growing to the next level and beyond. Turbo growth cannot be achieved through the transactional leadership they have become accustomed to. Instead, turbo growth requires you to transform your organization, perhaps several times over, and that can only be done through what Dr. Qubein calls transformational leadership.

I've met owners who have effectively retired but don't know it. Their businesses are losing relevance in the market, but they're not making any moves to adapt. If you're no longer relevant, whether you know it or not, you're on the path to extinction. It's no different from hardening of the arteries, which can move people closer to a massive heart attack while they may claim to feel perfectly fine.

To become a transformational leader, you must be an authentic catalyst for profound ongoing change in the organization. This requires you to think differently about the organization and behave differently, behavior determined by your beliefs. All the work done in chapters 1 and 2 by Mazzetti and Matlock is part of the necessary preparation to become a transformational leader. Transformational thinking goes right to your beliefs about yourself: "Who do I need to be to get what I want?" Transactional thinking, by contrast, simply asks, "What do I have to do to get what I want?" It's behavioral with little regard for underlying beliefs.

Transactions remain the lifeblood of the organization. There is no organization without them. But if you are leading your organization to transactional success, you're not being as effective a leader as you could be. Your leadership repertoire will be too limited to ever get you to turbo growth.

You can spot transformational leaders merely by listening to their manner of speech. Transformational leaders teach and inspire. Transactional leaders instruct and direct. Transformational leaders are educators. They teach the *why*, while transactional leaders train people in the *how*. Transformational leaders will share wisdom about how to be. Transactional leaders will dispense information that tells people what to do. Ultimately, the difference between the two leadership styles amounts to the difference between training and education. Training is always a discrete program. Education is a lifelong process.

Transactional Leaders . . .	Transformational Leaders . . .
• deliver training as a program	• provide education as a process
• dispense information	• share education
• teach how	• teach why
• tell you what to do	• show you how to be
• go from the unknown to the known	• develop reason
• are in the calendar business	• are in the relationship business
• are creative in their profession	• are innovative in their profession

These are much more than mere fine distinctions. They are profound differences that wind up taking companies in very different directions, depending on the CEO's leadership orientation. If you listen to how a leader chooses to solve problems, you can tell whether that leader's focus is on a transactional fix or a transformational shift. A transactional leader will approach a problem logically, as an unwelcome bump in the road that needs fixing. A transformational leader approaches the same problem in terms of what may need to change in the problem area. Every problem is viewed as a signal, a prompt to challenge assumptions and reconsider what the organization might miss if the problem were simply fixed on a transactional basis.

BUILDING A LEARNING ORGANIZATION

An organization led by a transformational leader is a learning organization, with the leader as the head teacher. In a learning organization, the leader helps everyone understand the *why* of what's to be accomplished, aligned with the leader's personal mission and vision for the organization. Transformational leaders use this orientation for long-term advantage, as a way to attract and retain top talent and build a loyal management team. Transactional leadership has the opposite tendency. It attracts transaction-oriented employees who are not likely to stay around for long.

Transformational leadership is predicated on relationship building, client loyalty and brand insistence (the expression of the brand at every client touch point). That is simply not achievable with transactional leadership, which is oriented toward filling the calendar, filling orders, client service, and brand awareness that drives more orders. Associates can be trained how to interact with clients with scripts, tools, and techniques, but unless those associates learn the *why* of the business, their interactions with clients will tend to be static and unsatisfactory.

Again, there is nothing inherently wrong with this. Every day I receive perfectly satisfying service from transactional companies. But I feel no loyalty toward these companies, and I presume they feel little loyalty toward me.

Transformational leadership expresses itself in a bias toward learning and relationship building throughout the business. For every business problem, there are alternative transactional and transformational courses for action. The transactional approach puts the emphasis on fixing the problem, while the transformational approach explores the growth opportunity presented by the problem.

Transactional leadership is more likely to makes cuts to achieve profitability, while transformational leadership is more likely to make investments—in new markets, in new products, in employee development and recognition, in employee retention, in new equipment, in product quality, in work processes, in support systems, in communications.

Both approaches are likely to achieve efficiencies and raise returns, but the transformational approach has an important advantage. Transformational leadership prepares the company much more thoroughly to improvise, adapt, and overcome. Transformational leadership prepares for the uncertainty and industry disruption in the years to come. Nimbleness, agility, innovation—all the necessities of twenty-first-century business success—are built into transformational leadership.

PASSION AND PRODUCTIVITY

Chapter 2 was all about aligning your behaviors with your beliefs in order to achieve greater productivity. Transformational leadership provides you with the opportunity to align your productivity with your passions to achieve greater fulfillment in your life.

The people who are most open to developing themselves as transformational leaders are either successful transactional leaders who have reached a crisis point in their lives, or leaders who never really mastered or enjoyed transactional leadership in the first place. I'm thinking of Audree, a client of mine who disliked managing her business so much that she contemplated leaving the financial services field. Audree was an excellent financial advisor and her clients loved her. She had won multiple top advisor awards from *Barron's* magazine. Nevertheless, Audree knew she didn't enjoy running her firm because she felt she wasn't good at it. She concluded that she had two options: she should either sell the firm and leave the industry or make the financial sacrifice of taking on a partner more comfortable with management chores.

Through my work with Audree, she was able to take a third route. She hired a professional manager, someone skilled in operations and business development, to tackle all the chores that she didn't enjoy. This may seem like a simple, rational choice, but it took a tremendous amount of introspective work on Audree's part. Before she could identify the right person to carry out this role, she needed to gain much deeper self-knowledge about her fixed beliefs, her self-limiting beliefs, and her vision of the life she wanted.

In the several years since hiring a professional manager, Audree has become a transformational leader of her firm. She continues to win awards for her high client satisfaction rates, and *Barron's* has named her among the nation's top 100 female advisors. She has coupled productivity with passion by having a superefficient operation behind her; she enjoys the rare gift of coupling productivity with her passion for working closely with her clients and serving their needs.

I've met very few people for whom the transition from transactional to transformational leadership arrives naturally without serious introspective work, as was undertaken by Audree. I've had coaching clients tell me, "I don't want to be a teacher. I like what I'm doing." Having labored for so many years to master transactional leadership, they are comfortable in the role and don't care to learn a whole new way of leading. Especially for those leaders who have earned so many trappings of material success, it's human nature for them to prefer doing what's always worked.

It may seem like simple common sense to delegate whatever you don't enjoy doing. But if you continue to think transactionally and don't take your beliefs and passions into account, you're more likely to dump your least enjoyable duties on others and call that delegating. Without the commitment to be an educator as a leader, you're highly susceptible to handing off work to unprepared subordinates on an ad hoc basis. I think it's true for most places of work that associates are rarely trained in how to do the delegated tasks correctly, nor are they properly educated to perform the task in a way that's aligned with the company mission and values.

Oftentimes, when I hear CEOs complain that their staff are incompetent, I later discover that their perception merely reflects their company's highly transactional work processes. Haphazard, delegation-on-the-fly practices abound. Tasks are dumped on associates with no education about why the delegated work is important, no ongoing training to help the employee develop proficiency at the task, and no follow-up or incremental feedback from the supervisor. Uneven results are the natural result. When workers and clients alike complain about the company's poor overall performance, the CEO concludes the firm is filled with incompetent employees. In fact, it would be close to a miracle for unprepared, untrained, and dumped-on employees to produce stellar work.

The larger problem in such a scenario is that business owners with a fixed belief that the staff is incompetent will continue dumping instead of delegating because they don't really believe their people are worthy of further education and development. Their employees don't grow in their abilities because they're never appropriately assigned and taught more challenging tasks.

It's a classic case of how a transactional leader's lack of self-awareness generates self-fulfilling prophecies. If you believe that your subordinates are incompetent, you will unconsciously find ways to support that belief. Delegation by dumping inevitably leads to employee dissatisfaction and high turnover, which can actually give a business owner further evidence that the staff is unworthy of training and education!

The immediate, practical function of delegating is to get non-productive tasks off your plate. But its most important overriding purpose is to develop leaders to lead on your behalf as you grow your company. For transformational CEOs, delegation becomes a repeatable strategy for freeing more and more of their time to execute their passions and strengths, rather than a tactical ploy to rid themselves of headaches.

Truly effective delegation only happens when the staff is educated on how to think about the task they've been given, aligned with how the leader of the organization thinks about the task. As you teach the *how* and the *what* of a task, it's important to explain the premise and the *why* behind the task. Stories and past examples of how the task makes a difference for other people—either clients or teammates—always help staff members make that critical mental connection between the task at hand and its impact.

Once you've chosen people with the talent and skill sets to do the job, it's up to you to teach them the *why:* the premise, and the thinking consistent with the values and tenets that make up your company culture. Then, when problems arise, the team can provide solutions in your absence, following the same execution philosophy that you taught them.

Educating your team along these lines and setting this standard for delegation creates a highly productive work environment, builds team cohesion and loyalty, and eliminates costly mistakes and rework. And when mistakes happen, they represent authentic learning opportunities. By turning over a portion of your responsibilities in this way, daily execution contributes to your company's evolving culture of learning—just one of the many force multipliers that will set your organization on a turbo-growth trajectory.

You'll begin to identify your passions from your vision board and from all the work you've done rethinking, reframing, and refocusing your beliefs. You'll also look for your passion to reveal itself, connecting you with something bigger and more important than your immediate wants and needs.

Have you ever stayed up late to complete a job that most people would put off until the following day? Have you had a long, hard day and found yourself energized instead of exhausted? These are clues to where your passions lie. Sometimes passion shows up inexplicably. You respond to an unusual challenge or sudden contingency with little self-conscious thought, seemingly by instinct. Later, you stand back and say, "Wow, I can't believe I just did that." What may have felt like instinct was the sensation of total immersion in your passion.

It is through your passion that you discover your purpose in life, the vision of your ideal self that calls you toward the highest and best in yourself. Turbo growth is built upon a three-legged stool: your vision and purpose, which point the direction of your growth; your results, which measure and fund your growth; and this combination of passion and productivity, the engine that drives your growth.

The trick is to find a sweet spot, a workable balance between passion and productivity. This is as true for your business as it is for all the other areas of your life. Productivity is easier to measure and manifest than passion. You can see it in action as you chip away at your to-do list and see the number of unchecked items go down. It can be measured in terms of new prospects, new business obtained, client goals being achieved, projects completed ahead of time. Productivity is so much more easily measured that it can easily crowd out passion. That's where effective delegation comes in as your strategy for protecting your passion from overwork.

Try this exercise. List the three activities that you would consider A-level or top-shelf activities. These are your most fulfilling activities, the ones that generate the highest upside for you, that you are most passionate about and create the greatest value for others. Then write out at least one action step (preferably two) that you plan to take in the next ten days to hit the passion and productivity buttons for each. Be as specific as you can. Vague responses will only dampen your results.

Now go back and do the same for three of your B-level or midshelf activities. These are the activities in the areas of your greatest competencies, where your reputation rests. They are profitable and doing them excites you. Write at least one action step to take in the next ten days for each that will maximize your efforts to spend time and energy on B-level activities.

Many of my clients are resistant when they see this deceptively simple and powerful exercise. They tell me, "I don't know why I should fill this out. I know what my A-level and B-level activities are, and I know I'm not doing them enough." What they don't recognize (until they've done it) is how putting them into words committed to paper can be extremely motivating. You probably know what's keeping you from the activities that give you the most fulfillment and generate the greatest profits, but you've avoided taking measures to change the situation. So, I tell the naysayers to take ten minutes and do this exercise. Consider that you're in a rut, and this might be the first step toward getting you out. Seeing your responses on paper can set you free to make room in your life for the things that mean the most to you.

SIGNIFICANCE AND SERVANTHOOD

The promise of significance awaits all human beings, although the word means something different to each individual. Your own definition of the term may elude you until you've engaged the same passion and productivity equation that fuels your business growth. Many have achieved great success through sheer productivity, but no one ever achieves significance until productivity is coupled with passion.

Earning, Learning, and Serving

We all know the time value of money: a dollar invested today will earn more interest than a dollar invested tomorrow. Let me introduce what I call the time value of life. If we start living the life we want today, we will enjoy a greater return on life than if we put it off until tomorrow. Our time, counted in the days we each have remaining, is a far more precious commodity than money. When we put off living our *why* for another day, another week, or another year, there are opportunity costs measured in unhappiness, emptiness, and regret.

As you read coming chapters, consider what kind of significant contributions you want to make to others, and not just in financial terms. Your significance is defined by the positive impact and influence you have on others, based on your leadership. For me, significance equals legacy, impact, and purpose and is guided by the pursuit of purpose and passion that feeds fulfillment every minute of the waking day. Significance can be measured by the lessons you learn and pass on as a teacher, in the present, in the future, and beyond your lifetime.

Consider some of these indicators of excellence in teaching. Each one also pertains to transformational leadership, guided by your passion and purpose in leading a life of significance:

- A good teacher, first and foremost, sees each student as an individual with hopes, dreams, strengths, and vulnerabilities.

- A good teacher nourishes and inspires.

- A good teacher makes learning exciting and fun, helping each student find areas of interest to explore and master.

- A good teacher constantly reminds students that mistakes are part of learning.

- A good teacher works to create a classroom atmosphere in which the guiding principle is that all students respect their fellow students and feel safe to share their thoughts and feelings.

- A good teacher creates a learning environment in which mistakes are opportunities for learning, and no students should ever feel embarrassed to ask questions if they do not understand something.

- A good teacher knows each student's academic strengths and needs, and even more about the interests, fears, hopes, and worries of each student.

- A good teacher helps students learn about themselves and learn about each other's strengths, hopes, and dreams.

- A good teacher remembers that each student is somebody's precious child, and that every parent has high hopes, valid concerns, and great expectations for that child.

- A good teacher tries to see things through the students' eyes as well, working hard to be fair, empathetic, and encouraging.

- A good teacher strives to maintain high expectations for each and every student, to challenge all of them to reach for their best and aim for the stars.

- A good teacher is strong, firm, and determined, showing students that learning and doing their best are the goals and that grades are not.

- A good teacher helps students see that goals that are at first difficult may eventually become easy and are often the most satisfying to achieve.

- A good teacher helps students view new things as stimulating challenges rather than dreaded obstacles.

- A good teacher shows students that perfection is not only unrealistic but undesirable.

- A good teacher becomes attached to the students, realizing that even if they never see each other again after their time together is done, students carry memories of their teachers into the future, where what they learned has an impact on their adult lives.

Although teachers are typically assumed to be authority figures, the list above reflects how so much of teaching is a noble form of servanthood. All educators teach in service to their students' aspirations and dreams. Most working professionals, years after grammar school or high school, will still cite the one or two teachers who fostered in them their love of what they do, and credit those educators for making their accomplishments possible.

Much the same can be said of transformational leaders in the memories of their employees, as servants to those employees. The most beloved leaders are often remembered by past employees as those who inspired them to achieve beyond what they thought they ever could.

Significance is about serving others before serving yourself, making your personal agenda secondary to those you choose to serve through your leadership. It is attached to a positive inner feeling you are intentionally trying to create in others as you serve them. Your followers feel you have touched their hearts and stirred their souls with your leadership, which helps them achieve their desired results.

In this sense, you can measure your significance by the lessons you learn and pass on. Guided by your purpose and passion, you will feed your sense of fulfillment every minute of the waking day.

A lot of entrepreneurs I know look back and marvel at what they've accomplished in the previous ten years. Very little of it was planned, most will readily concede. They put one foot in front of the other, through the ups and downs of the economy, and through disruptive forces in their industries, and ended up in a better place than they had imagined. Some have succeeded beyond their wildest dreams.

Think of your own past ten years. Take stock of how far you've come. Consider all the progress you've made in spite of whatever fixed beliefs and self-limiting beliefs you've discovered by reading this far. Now imagine looking forward to the next ten years. Think of your vision board and all the other tools you now have at your command for turning your core beliefs into actions and results.

EXERCISE 3.1
What's Your Personal Vision for Your Next Ten Years?

- What do you want to see when you look back ten years from now?

- What are you doing today to make that happen?

- What kind of impact will you have on others over the next ten years?

- How do you plan to serve others over the next decade?

- Whom do you want to impact the most?

- How do you want to impact each one of them?

- What will your legacy be?

- What lessons do you want to pass on?

If you remain mindful of the time value of life, you will recognize that the next ten years are coming anyway. So why not plan to live a life of significance and transformational leadership in those coming ten years?

It's up to us, as business leaders, to recognize that everything we think about is projected into our future and also into the future of our organizations and their people. Life is not about finding ourselves; it's about creating ourselves. And when we create ourselves, it's our privilege to create businesses that reflect our purpose and passions and provide them as gifts to employees in the form of transformational culture, the subject of the next section.

EARNING, LEARNING AND SERVING
Three Questions

The Mindset
What can you do to become a better transformational leader?

The Practice
Where will you swap C-level and D-level activities for A-level activities today?

The Opportunity
Where will you use an opportunity to teach and be a servant leader today?

PART TWO

The Cultural Excellence Officer

CHAPTER FOUR

Cast a Long Shadow

My eleven-year-old daughter often makes jewelry for sale at Studio Slant, the art gallery and gift shop my wife owns and runs in our hometown of Owensboro, Kentucky. Among the items she makes are those simple little bracelets marked "WWJD" (What would Jesus do?).

For Christians, these bracelets are a source of ongoing inspiration, reminding us of how we can solve our daily moral or ethical choices just by imagining what choice Jesus might make.

Sometimes I'll ask my daughter to make a set of custom bracelets in this style. For the *J*, though, I ask her to substitute the first-name initial of one of my coaching clients. The bracelets are meant to be distributed to his team: WWFD (What would Fred do?).

Blasphemy? Far from it. The purpose is similar, but it's adapted to a business setting. If everyone on Fred's team were to wear WWFD bracelets, they'd have constant reminders that in moments of indecision or hesitation, the best choice is to go with what they think Fred would do.

For Fred, though, those bracelets represent something much more important. They're a reminder to him of what a great responsibility he holds as the company's leader. The example he sets by his everyday choices and behaviors had better be good ones because they are always being interpreted and replicated by his team.

In any organization, people naturally try to follow in the leader's footsteps. If those footsteps are shaky or keep switching directions, you can expect the organization to do the same. But companies with leaders who are decisive and able to communicate their values and goals in an inspiring way that is easily understood by everyone are where you will find a company culture capable of tackling the challenges created by turbo growth.

As a leader, you can't expect people to step outside their comfort zones if you're not willing to do the same. That's the lesson Louis Gerstner learned when he led the big turnaround of IBM in the 1990s. When he was first named CEO, Gerstner relied on his consulting background to save billions of dollars through cost cutting and asset sales, but that wasn't enough to fix the company. To overcome IBM's hidebound bureaucratic culture, Gerstner discovered he had to get out of the corner office, where he was most comfortable, and spend thousands of hours making personal appearances as a cheerleader for IBM's new, nimble, growth culture.

"The thing I have learned at IBM is that culture is everything," Gerstner said in a talk at Harvard Business School in 2002.[6] No matter how smart your strategy is, the company's sense of shared values and identity will determine whether the strategy succeeds. "It took me to age fifty-five to figure that out," Gerstner said. I hope it doesn't take you that long to figure out culture is everything.

You will know your company culture has arrived when people are making decisions not just on the short-term tactical level but also from the philosophical standpoint of thinking as you do. That's pretty

---

6. Martha Lagace, "Gerstner: Changing Culture at IBM: Lou Gerstner Discusses Changing Culture at IBM," December 9, 2002, *Working Knowledge,* blog, Harvard Business School, accessed March 1, 2021, https://hbswk.hbs.edu/archive/gerstner-changing-culture-at-ibm-lou-gerstner-discusses-changing-the-culture-at-ibm.

awesome, but it also puts an awesome responsibility on you to identify what you believe and make those beliefs known to your team.

In part 1 of this book, you learned, as a chief executive officer, how to align your behaviors with your beliefs and then how to align your productivity with your passions.

Now in part 2, it's time for you, as a cultural excellence officer, to learn how to communicate your beliefs and your passions to your team in a way that instructs and inspires *their* behaviors and *their* productivity. This is the foundation of a strong and focused company culture, poised and ready for turbo growth.

As a leader, you need a team to follow through on all your intentions and priorities when you're not around. In essence, you want to duplicate yourself, so that everyone is able to intuit your wishes and make the same choices you would make. As a cultural excellence officer, you should nurture your company's culture as an extension of yourself, as a projection of your own personal values, vision, and sense of mission.

This section represents an enormous opportunity for you and your company. Based on all the work you've done in part 1, now you'll discover how to share it with others on your team so you're all pulling in the same direction, the direction that represents your goals for yourself, your family, your entire life. The goal is to build the best life you can imagine for yourself, and then build your company around it.

A lot of people get that backward, don't they? They sacrifice for their work, attempt to succeed at the expense of their personal life, and then try to make a personal life outside work that represents their true selves. In many respects, that's doing everything the hard way.

But don't get me wrong. This path is hard work, too. In some ways, it's much harder. You will need to go deeper, to draw out your personal beliefs and desired daily behaviors in a way that can be understood as values in action. Before you can even begin to build a great culture with your team, you have to do a lot of work on yourself, which is the subject of this chapter.

You need to take stock of your personal resources, and how you're deploying them, how you understand what you value most, and even how you manage your energy. Leaders who allow their energy to be depleted by difficult people and unaddressed problems are letting down the entire company.

At D2, everyone understands that our mission is to help people double their business in three years with half as many clients. They understand that our vision is to help advisors create extraordinary practices and extraordinary lives. And we do these things with these shared values: results first, excellence, integrity, service, education, and innovation.

That's the underpinning of our culture at D2. It's the result of years of hard work, which began with me. I personally had to do a lot of work on myself before any aspects of our mission, vision, and values could come into view and be made real for everyone else. By the same token, maintaining the authenticity of the mission, vision, and values is dependent on how well I live those values every day.

TAKE STOCK OF YOUR PERSONAL CAPITAL

Once you accept the premise that your company is an extension of yourself, you also must accept that the company's growth and development depend on your own personal growth first, and then the growth of your team. How can your team learn new things from you if you're not learning new things? How can they change and grow if you're not changing and growing?

The place to begin with personal development is to take stock of what I'd call your personal capital. This is the storehouse of personal assets you can deploy to get things done. As Dr. Qubein says, these assets fall roughly into four categories: relational, financial, educational, and reputational.

By taking stock of these four areas of personal capital, you'll see how efficiently you're using the assets you have at hand, and which of these assets need more attention and investment. Again, these are not self-improvement or self-help tips. They constitute a process of auditing your personal resources and finding opportunities for better uses, all for the benefit of your personal life and the business you're building around that life.

Relational Capital

Begin by identifying the people you know you want to spend more time with. Who in your world do you wish you could see more often, and in what creative ways can you make that happen? If you know them well enough to want to be around them, you probably know what they care about most. What could you do to show them you care about what they care about? It could be as simple as making sure you're a part of whatever charitable cause they're involved with; putting them on a regular routine for coffee, lunch, or dinner; participating in fun activities they enjoy; offering your talents to them, their kids, or business, and so on. The best offerings are based on what you know is important to the people you want to spend more time with.

For instance, my wife and I make it a habit to get involved in the activities our children take an interest in. It's important for us to have our kids know we support them. Whether it's coaching a sports team, volunteering on a board, lining up pregame meals for the team, getting costumes for a community theater production, speaking on career day at school, chaperoning school trips, or taking guitar lessons together, my wife and I want to show our support.

Now consider the people whom you feel you *need* to know. These are people who can open important doors for you, if only they knew you better. They're traveling in circles you want to be a part of. How can you get access to them? Have you even tried?

The fact is most of our relationships happen almost coincidentally. We feel comfortable developing relationships in that way, but comfort is not the road to growth. If you were to look at your relational capital as you would any other capital stock, you would see how you're missing chances for investments in valuable relationships that could be mutually beneficial, both personally and for your business.

Several of my clients are very deliberate in this way. They make lists of colleagues, presenters, and leaders they want to get to know at upcoming conferences. In coaching sessions, I've helped them plot out their course to engage and brainstorm with anyone they already know who can give them an introduction. We have identified those in their community they want to get to know for professional and personal reasons. Identifying people who have blazed the path you desire, meeting them, and learning from them is a great way to help boost your professional development, build a stronger network, and in some cases, grow your business.

Finally, remember the example you're setting for your team. If you want your company culture to be one of reaching out and building bridges to people who can help the company, you need to develop that skill yourself, work at it, demonstrate it, tell your team about it, and mentor them in doing it themselves.

Financial Capital

The old saying goes that the shoemaker's children go barefoot, and in a similar sense, many people in financial services don't handle their personal finances in ways that best reflect their personal goals and their goals for their businesses.

Have you identified a dollar target for the reserves you need to keep on hand? Have you hit that target, or is it just a pipe dream? If you haven't, why not? Do you have long-term savings? Do you know what you're going to do with the extra money you make this year?

What investments in the business are you deferring or just putting off indefinitely? Which investments in your personal life are being neglected the same way? More importantly, how did you determine how much to take out of your business this year?

I've seen extremes of both cases when it comes to this last question. I've seen business owners starve their businesses of growth and investment just to feed their lavish lifestyles, and I've seen the opposite: business owners who avoid investing in themselves and their personal growth because they keep putting money into growing their business.

Neither one of these approaches creates personal fulfillment. In both cases, owners have their lives and businesses too far out of alignment to ever achieve the optimal growth they desire: personal growth *and* growth in the business. It's very important that you, as a financial advisor, walk the talk. It's hard to take fitness advice from a flabby, out-of-shape trainer, and it's just as hard to accept financial advice from someone whose own relationship to financial and personal well-being is very questionable.

Educational Capital

Lifelong learning was always a good idea, but the speed of change in today's business environment now makes it an absolute necessity. If you're not learning, you're silently atrophying and growing ignorant.

Take stock of the things you wish you knew more about. Where can you learn these things, short of going back to school? Online learning is certainly convenient, but perhaps the better option is to develop local learning resources that your whole team can learn from. For example, many of my clients listen to Ted Talks when they work out, play audiobooks on car rides, keep an interesting book in every bathroom, invest in two or three conferences a year, take classes online for fun activities, and join mastermind groups to get help from their peers with challenges they face. All of this and more keeps them on a path of lifetime learning.

I encourage my clients to learn something new every year where their passion for the activity is high, but their skill set and competency are low. This kind of exercise helps build your learning muscles. Psychologist Angela Duckworth has said in her book *Grit*[7] that finding a new interest like this and then deepening it with practice can lead to developing a purpose and hope around that interest.

This helps you build grit, and it lets you expand your educational capital and your relational capital at the same time, another chance to create some intentional congruence.

Education is such a broad subject: you have existing skills you can fine-tune, new skills you want to challenge yourself with, and then there are your undernourished talents that have gone years without professional training.

I've recently taken up lessons in song writing and guitar playing. Did I have extra time for that? At first glance, no, of course not! But the

---

7. Angela Duckworth, *Grit: The Power of Passion and Perseverance* (New York: Simon & Schuster, 2016).

proficiency I'm developing in learning these skills is nurturing my soul and fulfilling my need to create. I am learning to become more efficient with multiple work items and shift my community involvement to make room for these new priorities.

As a leader, I know this new hobby of mine inspires my team and clients as they watch me take on some very unfamiliar and difficult new skills and confess my ignorance and clumsiness as a relative beginner. Many of my clients have told me that my explorations into music have inspired them to take on hobbies of their own. They're going to see live music more often, and some have taken voice lessons or are learning to play an instrument for the first time. Others have dusted off old instruments they've ignored for years and begun grooving again.

Any kind of new activity you pursue will open up a range of fresh opportunities for intentional congruence in your business. Thanks to the contacts I've developed on the Nashville music scene, I've begun hosting special music events for clients. I brought in two professional songwriters to teach clients how to write a song as a team-building exercise, and I hired a vocal coach who gives workshops teaching leadership through singing. One of our most popular events was led by singer-songwriter Jeffrey Steele, who's been inducted into the Nashville Songwriter's Hall of Fame and twice been named BMI Songwriter of the Year. Jeffrey spent an evening with our clients telling tales about entrepreneurship in the music business, and then he serenaded us with some of his fifteen number-one hits.

These were all unique, memorable events that earned rave reviews from our clients. None of them would have happened if I hadn't been determined to stretch myself personally and learn something new.

Reputational Capital

This seems to be the hardest capital stock to build on because your reputation exists in the minds of other people. Reputation has been defined as what people say when you're not around. How do you control that?

The natural starting point for increasing your reputational capital is to take an inventory of what makes you special, what already distinguishes you in your marketplace. You want to build a strong and specific reputation in your industry so people will think of you often for what you're good at. The thing that sets you apart is the thing that sets you free. It gives you freedom of movement, freedom to be fully expressed, and the privilege of building a reputation that springs from what you want to be known for.

I was once at a certification class where a younger financial advisor told me and a few other people that he wanted to be Travisesque in his personal leadership style. It was just about the best compliment I'd ever received because it told me that he got me for exactly who I am and what I want to communicate as my personal brand, and as my company's brand.

Do people think about you in terms that make you special? If not, why not? It's likely you're not deploying your reputational capital in the best way possible. Take a look at your current reserves of relationship capital, financial capital, and educational capital. How can you use some of your capital in each of those three areas to help build up your reputational capital?

In a professional environment, consider the rules of engagement that you apply to yourself in terms of building your reputation. It is inevitable that however you present yourself professionally, your team members will take the cue from you. And when someone strays from the reputation you want to uphold for the entire company, your own reputation will be essential to restating and enforcing the company's cultural norms. Within your company, the stronger your image and reputation, the easier it will be for your team members to emulate your intentions when making decisions.

Out-of-town events are occasions where many company reputations have been shaped and sometimes broken. Some companies have well-earned reputations for being *Animal House* partiers, and I've been adamant that to avoid even the slightest rumor of poor behavior, we need to control our alcohol consumption, stick together at social events, and return to our rooms at a reasonable time. Above all, we must never go out with clients after the event unless we decide to do so *as a group*.

Early in my career, a young lady new to our team and only a few years removed from college traveled to a workshop with us. Although we were clear about these rules, she disappeared during an after-hours event and was seen, by several people, leaving with two male clients.

When we all called it a night, we couldn't locate her, and she wasn't responding to our texts or phone calls. We got worried and continued this pursuit for a few hours with no response. The following morning she finally responded, saying that she had gone out with a few of our clients, and she didn't know why we were so concerned.

When I asked her how she thought it looked to leave the bar with two men, it started to sink in.

When she hadn't responded to our texts or calls, and we asked around about anyone seeing her, our clients were the ones telling us she had left with two men. A few clients commented that this didn't look good for her or our firm. Those comments stung. Just like that, I could feel my own reputation and my firm's reputation take a hit.

All employees are expected to act as adults, so I would never compare this situation with child rearing, but your company culture does require the kind of nurturing you would give to a child.

Your child needs direct boundaries and clear consequences, and above all, your child looks to you to set the example.

My wife and I have been very open with our teenage son about the challenges he faces as he becomes a young man. Teaching him to mind his reputation for how he treats others, especially members of the opposite sex, was paramount for us from the time he was in middle school. My wife, Christy, would tell him before school dances and other social functions to do three things to stay out of trouble: "Keep your tongue in your mouth, hands in your pockets, and your penis in your pants." If some of my son's friends were in the car on the way to the event, they'd hear the message, too.

Memorable and direct advice of that kind, delivered with a sense of humor, is what it takes to make an impression. Maybe you find yourself teaching your kids philosophies and behaviors that are important to you. You can also reflect on what your parents, teachers, coaches, and mentors taught you as you were growing up. These lessons and the application of them tie directly into your reputation.

The reputational capital you build as your company's cultural excellence officer will be drawn down in your role as client experience officer (part 3 of this book). Your reputation helps determine how you position yourself in your market, and your positioning, in turn, influences and monetizes the value of your reputation.

WE'RE ALL IN THE ENERGY BUSINESS

Every day, I check in with each of our team members. I'll often shake their hand, look them in the eye, and ask them, "How are you doing today?" I've got to gauge everyone's energy level on a daily basis. If someone's off, if there is low or negative energy, I'll stop and find out what's going on, not as a lengthy counseling session but just to take the temperature, to diagnose the symptoms. Depleted energy and negative energy are twin contagions. I can't afford to let negativity spread.

We're all in the energy business. Your responsibility as a leader is to provide the company with a continual flow of uplifting positive energy. Why? Because as the leader, you are the only one with the ultimate authority to address the sources of any negative energy that threatens to drag down your company.

The natural question then is: If I'm responsible for keeping everyone's energy levels high and positive, who's doing that for me? How am I supposed to maintain my high energy levels if negativity is so contagious?

Excellent question.

Draw a vertical line down the middle of a sheet of paper and on the right side, make a list of all the people who drain energy from you when you're around them. Look at each name and ask yourself how you might conserve your positive energy by limiting your exposure to them.

The most common of these energy vampires are those whose main operating mode is cynicism. They are pessimistic and suspicious, and their default is skepticism instead of possibility. Now, in certain roles in a company, suspicion and skepticism are valuable attributes; think of a comptroller or cybersecurity specialist, or anyone involved in security or compliance.

On the other hand, only some compliance officers have cynical, negative personalities to go with their skeptical natures. Many, if not most, compliance officers are pleasant and positive in outlook. They are not only very good at their jobs but also have the ability to make compliance a positive thing for the company, not a drag and a downer. The point is, having a job that requires skepticism does not excuse having a cynical personality.

Now, on the left side of the paper, make a list of all the people who *give* you energy. You feel energized after seeing these people. Even talking to them on the phone or getting texts or emails leaves you feeling uplifted.

Cynics have a way of bringing everyone down in the same way. But some people who make you feel uplifted may not have as strong an impact on me. So it's important for you to take a moment to write down why these people give you energy. Recall your last interaction and try to pinpoint what made you smile and feel full of possibility. If you're having trouble putting your finger on it, ask mutual friends if they feel the same and why.

You want to distinguish what makes them special. If you can do it, it's like striking oil or discovering any other energy source. You will gain a greater understanding of what fuel you run and what gets you the best mileage. Then you have a better idea of which people in your life you absolutely must spend more time around, and whom you might want to call when you need a lift. The fact is that people who are full of energy are full of life and possibility. You want to be around them because they have a vision for life that's bigger than their own self-interest.

The nineteenth-century writer Ambrose Bierce defined cynicism as a "defect of vision that sees the world as it is, instead of as it should be." Cynics will call themselves realists, but not because they're committed to gauging just how much change is realistically possible. They call themselves realists as an excuse to never change.

Your team is dependent on you as a source of energy, so you are dependent on everyone you're in contact with to not cut off your energy supply. Make another list. Write down all the things you can do to eliminate the time spent with those specific people who drain you.

80

Don't be "realistic" about this! Energy is so important to you that if you allow it to be drained, you're putting all your plans and visions at risk. If there's a big client who has a way of draining and depressing you and all your team members as well, maybe referring that client elsewhere is the healthiest thing you can do for yourself and your company. What about old friends on this list? Sometimes friends from your earlier years no longer fit in with you the way they once did.

When you do this exercise of assessing the people in your life in terms of energy gained and lost, it gives you a chance to see clearly who in your life actually supports your dreams and who doesn't. There really are right people and wrong people to have in your life. If people bring you down and prove to be consistent drags on your ability to stay positive, it's absolutely vital that you recognize the terrible consequences of maintaining those relationships.

These wrong people have a way of making you feel uninspired and unworthy, whether they mean to or not. Many feel stuck in their own lives and feel threatened by your presumption that positivity and hard work will change life for the better. They also may fear you'll abandon them if you get too big, so they try to pull you down instead. Whatever their reasons, they are sabotaging you, your business, and your dreams. You need to be clear about the risks of being around them and the vital importance of moving them out of your life.

KNOW YOUR VALUES

At least once a week, I get a call from an advisor who wants to hire me, but with this qualification: he doesn't want to go through all this work. He just wants to be tutored in all the mechanics of building a client experience timeline or streamlining back-office operations. On the rare occasions that I've counseled someone in just one practical aspect of our turbo-growth model, the results have never been good, and I'm not surprised.

Basically, these callers want me to help them build a house and skip the lessons on architecture. Because that's what this is. It's the architecture of success. A house that's built in ignorance of architecture will collapse. The destruction may not come today or tomorrow, but it will inevitably come under the stress of change and disruption.

If you have a deep understanding of why you want turbo growth for your business, you will welcome the challenges of being a teacher to your team members, of doing the hard work of building better relationships with the right people. You will be able to seek support from your heroes, gurus, mentors, and coaches, knowing that sometimes those requests will be turned down. When mind, body, and spirit come together, you are unstoppable because even setbacks become opportunities to learn and grow.

As leaders, we should all be doing four things constantly and with impeccable consistency:

- informing

- involving

- inspiring

- inspecting

Before we can succeed at any of these tasks with our teams, we must succeed at them with ourselves. In the course of building a strong company culture, we must be thoroughly informed about our own beliefs and values before we can lead others to disclose their own beliefs and values. We must involve ourselves in the lives of people we respect and admire before we can ask our team members to do the same. We must open ourselves up to be inspired and to follow our own passions before we can inspire passion in others. And we must never stop inspecting ourselves for integrity and consistency before we can do the same for our team members.

As a cultural excellence officer, you are going to lead your company's team members on an extraordinary journey in which the culture must endure the constant pressure of growing beyond your current capacities. To achieve this, you must persuade them that the change is worth it to them on a personal and professional level. You must encourage them to adopt the attitude that job security and career advancement is rooted in a company that is focused on growth. How will you do this if you are not clear about your own personal *why* as it relates to everything you're doing to grow the company?

When you've made these moves to lead yourself, you're ready to lead others on the path to turbo growth.

CAST A LONG SHADOW:
Three Questions
The Mindset
Of the four areas of personal capital,
how will you restock your most depleted area today?

The Practice
How will you maintain a higher level of energy today
that will inspire those around you?

The Opportunity
How will you put into action today all four key leader activities:
informing, involving, inspiring, inspecting?

CHAPTER FIVE

Shine a Bright Light

A few years ago, our financial planning firm was doing a periodic segmentation project to figure out how many clients we might sell to another firm because they no longer fit our long-term plans. The analysis showed that we should probably sell the account of a 100-year-old client with a $1 million portfolio.

That was a big portfolio, but we also knew that when this client passed away in the not-too-distant future, the portfolio would be divided among twenty beneficiaries. Preparing paperwork for all those beneficiaries would likely be a complex and time-consuming nightmare with little or no reward, because almost all of that money would leave the firm. It would be one of those tasks we'd do because we had to but would prefer to avoid if we could.

I agreed with the young associate heading the segmentation project that selling the account would make perfect business sense. But in that moment, as a leader, I also saw a coaching opportunity.

I started asking the young associate a series of questions about integrity, one of our firm's core values. This client had been with us for forty years, I reminded him. Did it show integrity on our part to cast off a legacy client because of her advanced age? Were we really living the value of integrity if we rewarded her years of loyalty to us by selling her account to someone else?

Personally, I was certain that keeping this client was the right thing to do. Selling the account would violate our values, and I would feel terrible about doing so. But rather than make a ruling as the boss, I wanted to have a conversation with the associate, as a coach and mentor. I wanted him to think it through, recognize the values at play on his own terms, in the context of our team culture. We had a memorable conversation that I think gave us a refreshed sense of why we're in this business, and why we love what we do.

A few weeks later, I relayed this conversation during one of our monthly team meetings and made it a learning opportunity for everyone. I wanted them to understand how this relatively minor choice involving a single client defined our culture. We live integrity. This is who we are to our clients. This is why we exist as a company.

BUILDING A TEAM CULTURE

Conversations such as these are the product of years of work on developing a shared vision, mission, and values for the company. It's a process that begins with your reflections on your own personal vision, mission, and values as a person and as a leader. The company's shared vision, mission, and values, however, should be the product of a team effort. Building a team culture must involve the team in the process or it's not likely to take. Few of your employees will be inspired by the prospect of giving you a great life. The vision, mission, and values must be larger than you, larger than any single person, in order to inspire the teamwork necessary to get the work done.

At Bob Bonfiglio's financial planning firm, Rise Private Wealth Management, the work on culture began with a team retreat on the subject of values. All the company's employees were prompted to name their five or six most important personal values, and then, with all the values up on a big board, they began to look for commonalities among team members. Certain values had different words but very similar meanings. "We kind of whittled it down," Bob recalled in an interview, "and over the course of probably two or three months at different team meetings, we came up with the six values we have now." Those six team values are integrity, health, family, client-focused service, growth, and philanthropy.

Out of those values came the mission statement and vision statement. The mission, the team decided, should be a simple and memorable declaration that embodies what the team provides to clients. "We actually wanted to get it down to three or four words," Bob said. "Compliance made us add a few more." The mission statement reads: "Financial advice that brings you confidence, simplicity and success."

The vision statement took a while to arrive at, over at least six months of meetings. The team kept seeking the right words that would represent a stretch, something for them to aspire to that would not be very easily attained. The vision is: "To be the most referred and recognized wealth management practice in the industry with a strong community presence."

Five years later, these values and statements continue to inform and inspire the working culture at Bob's firm. Their words appear in big graphics on the office walls and every employee is issued credo cards with mission, vision, and values on them. The mission, vision, and values are put on display before every team meeting. "People see the vision, we talk about the vision and how we're living the values," Bob said. "So, we know they're alive and well." At each annual leadership meeting, they're all reviewed, just to check if they're still valid and still driving the company culture.

The 3 CEOs

A common challenge faced by every entrepreneur—and this bears repeating—is that your success depends upon people on your team whose ideas about success *differ* from yours. After all, if your employees all thought as you do, they'd be running their own companies, not working for your company.

This is why so many entrepreneurs fail at being leaders. They get frustrated by the vast chasm between employee mindset and entrepreneurial mindset. They measure their people by their own capabilities. They'll say, "Wait a minute, how come they're not thinking like me? How come they're not committed like me? How come they're not going after it with the same zest and zeal as I do?" Either they don't grasp the inevitable difference in employer-employee mindsets, or they don't want to be bothered doing the work to breach that divide.

Shared culture is the only way to get people with very different mindsets into the same boat and rowing together toward common goals. It can be hard work to discover the common values that are right for your team, but the effort is well worth it.

When we did the exercise listing our top five personal values at D2, my personal top five were leadership, integrity, creativity, family, and health.

Only two other people included leadership as a top value, and only one other team member listed creativity. That's fine because what was more important was commonality. Integrity, family, and health were extremely common shared values, and that gave us something to build on. The other thing to consider was the wide diversity of powerful values that represented each team member's unique contribution, including empathy, excellence, service, fairness, loyalty, friendship, faith, grace, laughter, growth, connection, excellence, fun, joy, compassion, and authenticity.

As I read this list, I feel moved by how all of these personal values contribute to our shared culture at D2. It's the beautiful mosaic out of which our six company values emerged: service, integrity, innovation, education, excellence, and results.

Yes, I want D2 team members to have the understanding of WWTD (What would Travis do?) throughout the day. But it's even more important that they work together around these shared values, and with respect for each other's unique gifts and attributes.

CULTURE IS A PROCESS

A winning culture is about learning, about sacrifice, about serving your teammates. Coaches who build winning cultures are the coaches with organizations that win year after year. Why? Because tactics and techniques are so much easier to teach when they are embedded in a coherent set of beliefs and values, capped with a rallying cry. In terms of mindset, it's the difference between going through the motions—what I call low-velocity thinking—and making an effort toward breakthrough results, with full understanding of the mission and the vision.

The big advantage we had in football was the game tape. I learned to love film sessions because even when I thought I'd had a great game, the video would show that if I graded out at an 88 percent, which was high, it still meant I hadn't done my job on 12 percent of my plays. It was brutal, sometimes, to see myself fail like that and have a coach point out the mistakes, but it was also a great way to learn.

We don't have game tapes in the workplace, which makes culture building all the more important. You have to continually trust your teams with assignments for which they don't know the answer in advance. They have to figure it out. Let's see how they react. Let's see what they come up with on their own. It's a leadership principle I call trial by fire, because if you want your teams to be an extension of you, there are times you want them figuring out things completely on their own, without ever asking you to make decisions for them or express your preferences.

At our company, all the team members know not to come to me with a problem unless they've exhausted every other avenue trying to find a solution. That kind of cultural effect doesn't happen overnight inside a company. People are naturally afraid to make a decision and then risk being reproached later with "Why didn't you come to me first before doing this?" It takes a lot of trial and error, a lot of back and forth. You've got to be patient. You've got to let people fail. That's trial by fire.

Failure represents a learning opportunity only if the failure occurs while exercising company values. In terms of my own company's values (service, integrity, innovation, education, excellence, and results) it's reasonable to say that if you failed while exercising these values, if you were honestly trying to innovate with integrity, service, and results in mind, then you likely learned from it. That's a big part of leadership that entrepreneurs might not grasp if they haven't done sufficient work on company culture.

It's the same with the broader subject of delegation. Without the strong glue of a positive, healthy company culture, delegating authority to a team can be disastrous because team members will all apply their own concepts of how to work together. They'll end up talking past each other, if not outright bickering and arguing to a standstill. Or worse, they'll stop communicating so that tasks start getting lost between the cracks.

Sometimes, when I see something that's a little out of step with our values, I may stop and make an observation, but only if it's an opportunity for some coaching. One day, I overheard an associate talking to a prospective client about scheduling. The client wanted to delay making a decision. The associate said something perfectly pleasant and very innocent such as "Let us know when you'd like us to reach out again," or "We'd love to have you as a part of the Dynamic Directions community whenever you're ready."

The trouble is that statement does not accurately reflect our culture when it comes to sales. We are selective about whom we accept as clients. I just shot her a quick note saying, "Hey, I appreciate what you're doing, but when you say, 'We would love to have you as part of the Dynamic Directions community,' that statement isn't true. We don't know yet whether they're a good fit."

Then I recommended some alternative phrasing the next time a similar circumstance came up: "Hey, we welcome the opportunity to run you through our due diligence process to make sure this is a good fit. Whenever you're serious about considering a coach, let us know so that we can see if we're compatible." That's the language I use, because one of the ways we differentiate ourselves in our marketplace is by not chasing people. It was important to me to take the time to talk about that subtle difference.

Monthly team meetings are critical for passing along stories of this kind so that everyone can benefit from the interaction. Several of the practices we coach take fifteen minutes at the start of monthly meetings for associates to share their stories of what they did to live the company's values in the previous month.

There is a shared language at our company, which I take as sign of a healthy culture because it allows action to take place quickly, with a deep, shared understanding of what certain terms mean. Everyone knows that when we ask, "What's our wow for this meeting?" we're referring to that certain wow item or activity that will make the gathering feel special and memorable. A recovery gift is what we send out with an apology when we've made a mistake with a client. Our company nickname for compliance is *business prevention*. We even have our own unique office expletive, a silly two-word phrase that sounds a little like *dad-gummit!* You'll hear someone say it when something's gone wrong; I won't repeat it because it's an inside joke that only D2 team members would get.

We are all also familiar with the Kolbe personality assessment test and understand how its four modes of operation apply to our team members. I'm a well-known *quickstart* because when I get an idea, I run with it. Other people are known variously as *fact finders, follow thrus* or *implementers*, indicating each of their preferred operational styles. We use these tags within our company culture not to pigeonhole people but to appreciate personality differences among our team members, and to assign tasks to them in ways that set them up for success.

Shared language at Bob's financial planning firm includes references to valued behavioral norms such as "Say what you're for, not what you're against," and "If you see a problem, propose a solution." That's a great way to generate productive feedback and prevent a culture of complaint from forming. Feedback of that kind is encouraged from everyone, whether intern or partner. Bob periodically takes interns out to lunch and urges them to point out things they believe aren't working well. "A leadership norm of mine is that the people closest to the work know the most about it," he said. The benefit is that everyone is in the habit of thinking up new solutions for the work they're assigned to, while developing their skills in the process.

CULTURE IS YOUR GROWTH ENGINE

These exercises around shared values and mission and vision statements need to be revisited on an annual basis because conditions change and (assuming you're growing) new team members and new function areas need to be a part of the ongoing evolution of the company culture.

For example, mergers and acquisitions, which are essential to turbo growth, can also create challenges for company cultures if they're done with too much emphasis on the bottom line, and not enough on cultural fit. You want to arrive at a set of processes and systems that are so well defined within your company culture that the culture perpetuates itself as it grows. Add just one bad acquisition to the mix, and the ill effects can ripple outward for years. Even worse, when you make an acquisition on the basis of how much revenue it will bring in, without proper regard for cultural fit, you risk communicating to your entire team what it is you really value most.

The culture at Bob's firm today is very high energy, with lots of teamwork, collaboration, and feedback. It's not for everyone. People who prefer to do their work and be left alone will not enjoy the culture there, and it's a mistake to hire such people. The key to maintaining a heathy culture in a growing company is to do a lot of due diligence before adding someone to the team. In Bob's interview process, job candidates are asked about their values. "If you're not in tune with the values of our team, we're just not going to get along," Bob said. "We don't want to waste everyone's time by hiring someone who's a poor fit, just because they're professionally well-qualified."

At the same time, it's irresponsible to put the focus on growing the company without supporting each team member's personal growth. At Bob's firm, there's a program called Internship to Partnership that helps team members grow in their career. There's a document that lays out very clearly what people need to achieve to be considered for the next level in their career at the company. In addition to an annual performance review, which is all about how well the employee is serving the company, there is a second career review that checks in with the employees and their career trajectory. It's a way of making sure the employees find their current roles fulfilling and have their eye on career stepping-stones. The idea is to make sure that career aspirations can be fulfilled inside the company over time so that the people who are acculturated with Rise Private Wealth Management are able to grow along with the company.

It takes a special kind of person to enjoy working in a company experiencing turbo growth. There's always something new to do that's never been done before, and you're constantly asked to stretch your capabilities. Some people thrive amid such uncertainty, while others wilt with fear and anxiety. Once you understand and accept that your company's culture isn't for everyone, it should make it easier to let go of people who can't keep up and don't enjoy trying. You owe it to everyone else in the organization to remove people who aren't a fit for the company culture. That's how you strengthen the culture and prepare it for its next wave of turbo growth.

SHINE A BRIGHT LIGHT
Three Questions

The Mindset
What are three things you can do today to get your company living your culture?

The Practice
What's missing on your shared language list?

The Opportunity
How can you use the highest-functioning aspects of your company's culture to dial up the velocity of thinking and follow-through within the organization?

CHAPTER SIX

Make a Firm Impression

One the most important tasks for anyone to complete under our coaching is a ten-year plan. When I introduce the idea, most clients are daunted by the concept. "Ten years?" they say. "Are you kidding? We don't know where the markets will be in ten *months*."

The point of a ten-year plan is not to predict the future. It's to set a trajectory for your company's turbo growth so you know what you need to be doing this quarter, next quarter, next year, and the year after in order to stay on track with your long-term goals. This plan also gives you a balanced approach to your decision making. With your short- and long-term goals laid out, a decision can be made on the merits of achieving both timeframes.

Although the worksheets for the ten-year plan are fairly simple and straightforward, they raise questions that are anything but. I began work one spring with a growing midsize partnership, and the weeks started rolling without either of the partners so much as touching the ten-year plan exercise. Thinking ten years ahead was too much for them. They had built their business by thinking six to twelve months out, and that was where all their horizons were set.

Slowly, they started chipping away at the ten-year plan worksheet, adding an item here and an item there after a lot of discussion. As the one-year anniversary of our work together approached, they finally completed it. All those months had been spent wrestling in their minds over what they wanted their business to be.

When they presented their plan to me, they were a little defensive about why it had taken so long. I remember one of them saying, "Look, we needed to go through what we needed to go through. This thinking was foreign to us. It was very hard, but now we see the value and merit in it."

I assured them what they had gone through was not meant to be a mechanical step-by-step process, even though it looks that way on the planning worksheet. A ten-year plan is an organic process like aging fine bourbon in a barrel or growing a beautiful garden. In this particular case, the two partners used the ten-year plan as an occasion for introspection about themselves and about what they wanted out of the business in ten years. Each had to shift certain personal beliefs and assumptions about themselves, about each other, and about the business before they could move forward far enough to even imagine where they'd want to be in ten years.

That takes time. It goes all the way back to how beliefs become thoughts and thoughts become actions. There were a number of tactical and strategic choices the two had to come to grips with before they could envision a long-term future together. The worksheet for the ten-year plan was an important catalyst. It created a sense of urgency for them to make a series of directional choices and set a trajectory that would motivate them in all their work going forward.

THE MAGIC OF A LONG-TERM VISION

Ten-year plans are just about the coolest thing I get to do with my clients. It's a kind of deliberate dreaming that forces them to see themselves ten years down the road and imagine what kind of life they want for themselves over the course of those ten years.

If culture is like the sheet music for your company (since it's now more like an orchestra than a rock band), then the ten-year plan supplies the beat. It sets the tempo of everything that happens every day, because it drives all your quarterly and yearly goals for growth and informs all your decisions for attaining those goals.

The ten-year-plan worksheet is a plain-looking, two-page questionnaire, but the formula for growth that comes out of each one is distinctive for every client, which is what makes it so much fun to work on. The clients all have their own ideas about what to add and how, as they would when choosing ingredients for a cake or marinade.

The first questions the ten-year plan asks concern your company's profile in ten years. What do you want it to look like? What services will your business provide? How many employees will you have? What will be your reputation in your community? How will prospective clients view you?

These questions may seem impossible to answer, but your responses will add a valuable layer of clarity in your day-to-day decision making. Sometimes I ask owners of midsize companies what they would have done differently ten years earlier had they known this was where they were headed. All of them agree that if they'd had this ten-year vision in their heads, they would have probably gotten a lot further. There's nothing you can do about a lesson like that except *learn* from it. Cast your vision ahead ten years, and if it gives you pause, recall how hard it would have been ten years ago to envision where you'd be today.

The 3 CEOs

When business owners start thinking in the long term, it gets them out of the tactical day-to-day mindset and helps them focus on what they really want to do.

Next comes your own role ten years down the road. What do you want to be doing? How is that role different from your role today? What needs to change for that to happen?

This question is one that a lot of people get stuck on. Most entrepreneurs build their life around their businesses. They're workaholics or "work-a-frolics" who just love to work and have work built into their lifestyle. They've got the entrepreneurial bug, and they're not sure they want a cure. But this kind of introspection is a great opportunity to flip the script and say, "If I'm going to build this business over the next ten years, how can I build it around my life and roles I want to play?"

Here is where very personal considerations arise, especially when it comes to family life. How much time to do you want to spend working and traveling for work during your children's middle-school and teenage years? How much freedom do you need to spend time with your family?

And then, if your kids are older, what do you want for life when the nest is empty? What kinds of interests would you pursue if you had the freedom, because you've built the business so well that you have a cohort of good people running it every day?

I think of myself, and our ten-year plan, and how there are some things I might want to be doing more of over the coming years: more travel, more public speaking, more music, perhaps getting back into theater. And then how will that affect my marriage, and what Christy wants for our time spent together?

If you aspire to be a true CEO—in all three meanings presented in this book—then these are the options you have for your life.

And if you're not there yet, the question becomes, "Well, what needs to be done differently? What should I start thinking about?"

The next question is what kind of revenue will you be bringing in ten years from now? How different is that from what you're making now? How will you get from here to there? This is where I often end up challenging people for thinking small. Our mission is help clients at least double in size over three years. If your company approximately doubles in size every three years, by the end of year ten, it should be at least ten times as large as it is today.

That question leads naturally to drawing up an imaginary organizational chart for what the company will look like in ten years. Most new coaching clients don't have a chart at all. Who does what is all kept in their heads, which is why they find it absolutely daunting to imagine what it would take to run a business ten times as large. Fundamental to your mapping out future growth is to draw up your current chart and then grow it out to correspond with your revenue goal.

Who are all those people in that chart? They're the people you haven't met yet, whom you're going to hire to duplicate yourself, over and over again, as you grow your company. Without a vision of that organizational chart that needs to be filled, how will you ever know who to search for? Now you can look at an entry level position with new eyes. What could this person be doing for you in ten years? Thinking big for yourself requires thinking big about your team members, and the ten-year organizational chart gives focus to that thinking.

Clientele is another area where I have to prod people to think in terms of bigger portfolios and fewer accounts. When people come across the ten-year plan, they might have no distinctive client niches, or maybe they have too many, ten or twelve of them, taking them in all different directions. A long-term plan helps them see the riches in their niches. They'll say, "This niche is my favorite, but my second favorite is where all the growth is. That's where I'd want to gravitate with my marketing." The niche could be doctors, engineers, or retirees in Florida. Niches can get very specific without becoming limiting at all.

EXERCISE 6.1
The Ten-Year Plan Worksheet

Profile
What will your business profile be in ten years? What service will your business provide, how long will you have been in business, how many employees will you have, what will your reputation be in your community, how will prospective clients view you, and so on?

Your Role
What will your role in your business be in ten years? How is that different from your current role? What needs to change for that to happen?

Revenue
What kind of revenue will you be bringing in ten years from now? How different is that from what you're making now? How will you get from here to there?

Organizational Chart
1. Draw a current organizational chart of your company.

2. Draw a future version of the organizational chart with the structure you would like to have in ten years.

Clientele
Write a description of what your client base will look like ten years from now.

1. Quantitatively: use relevant measures such as revenue per client, assets under management, and so on.

2. Qualitatively: what five adjectives would you use to define what your future client base will look like?

Action Questions

1. What are the three biggest challenges that could keep you from enacting your ten-year plan?

2. What are the three biggest opportunities you need to capture to help you achieve your ten-year goals?

3. What are the three biggest risks you need to manage as you pursue your ten-year plan?

This exercise is also available to download from our website: dynamicdirections-d2.com/the3ceos.

LEVERAGING THE TEN-YEAR PLAN

At the end of the ten-year plan, there are the three big action questions:

1. What are the three biggest challenges that could keep you from enacting your ten-year plan?

2. What are the three biggest opportunities you need to capture to help you achieve your ten-year goals?

3. What are the three biggest risks you need to manage as you pursue your ten-year plan?

Answering these three questions is where I've seen magic happen. Without fail, once clients get a vision of where they want to be in ten years, they encounter these questions and realize that the challenges they face are fairly familiar, the opportunities are enormous, and the risks are manageable.

Then they ask themselves, "Why should this take us ten years?"

What started out as an unimaginable dream—thinking a decade ahead—frequently becomes fodder for a five-year plan, and in some cases, a three-year plan.

As I went over one coaching client's plan with him, asking him about the challenges and risks that stood in his way, he said to me, "This is crazy. Why am I going to wait ten years for this? If this is where I want to be, I want to ask how I can get there in five years or less. There are some things here I could start doing right away. I don't have to wait at all." Seeing clients realize that what they thought was impossible is now possible is very rewarding for me.

I like to challenge my coaching clients in this direction because it really is true that once you can envision your ideal future, what had been previously almost unimaginable suddenly becomes the next obvious thing. And it's not just about growing the business; it's also about stepping back from unproductive workaholism, allowing your team to run the business while you're taking a long vacation. All of a sudden, the six- or eight-week vacation that seemed to be a ten-year goal gets added to next year's calendar.

For entrepreneurs, planning takes a shift in mindset, but not to slow them down or make their thinking more bureaucratic. The ten-year plan is a framework for their thought processes so they can cycle ideas through it, cycle opportunities through it, cycle decisions through it. Entrepreneurial thinking tends to be fast and furious, and the ten-year plan is just a vessel for steering all that energy in the direction of turbo growth.

As part of the ten-year plan, you created a start-doing list and a stop-doing list to inform your daily action items. To become a true

CEO, these are the things that will get you there. When you start with your ideal role in the organization and gain clarity about what that entails, you can grow your business around what you're trying to accomplish rather than having the business dictate what you must do. You'll ask, "How am I going to replace myself if I have 300 clients, and that could be 600 clients in a few years from now? If I'm giving up stuff along the way, who is going to pick that up within the organization?"

This work is necessary because short-term decision making will always tend to drag you into the weeds. You come to each decision now with a short-term plan and a long-term plan in mind. It could be a new hire, a new product, a new client niche, a new opportunity. If your choice fits both the short-term and long-term goals, you have an easy decision to make. But if it fits the short term and strays from the long term, or vice versa, then it's time to assess risks and rewards, all within the context of where you want to be in ten years. Maybe you sacrifice something in the short term because you see the long-term value. Or you turn down what seems to be a potentially lucrative opportunity, because even if it succeeds, it doesn't take you anywhere you want to go.

Even with a ten-year plan to guide you, it's easy to get distracted by smaller concerns. An owner might balk at some of the risks involved in a new acquisition, or in a real estate deal for a bigger headquarters. I'll be talking to a business owner about a great new idea for expanding the business, and I'll hear him say, "Well, I don't know if that will work."

I reply, "Really? We come up with a great idea and the first thing you want to talk about is how it's not going to work?"

Money concerns also come up early when we consider a growth idea before we've even considered the much more important points: Does this meet your mission? Does it meet your vision? Is it a fit for the culture? Will it lead to fulfilling the goals in your ten-year plan or will it distract from them?

Here's what happens at the time. When you ask yourself those questions and really dive in, a lot of ideas fail to make the cut. They're not a good fit for one reason or another, so money isn't an issue worth discussing. And for those ideas that do make the cut? If you have a growth idea that checks all these boxes and fits your ten-year plan, you will find the money. You will figure it out. It always works.

The ten-year plan takes you out of the weeds and gives you problems to solve: How are you going to meet your growth goals? What will it take? You focus your tactics and strategies on the numbers derived from the goals in your ten-year plan.

Spurring faster growth raises the tempo of work at the company and at times puts a strain on everyone. That's not a bad thing. Some people rise to the occasion. You realize you didn't know what they had in them until the imperative of growth caused them to stretch themselves.

From an employee retention standpoint, there's so much more to be gained when you have a ten-year plan that notifies everyone in the company where you're headed. Most important are the ones who buy into your vision and see prospects for their own personal growth and career development in your long-term plan. They are exactly the kind of people you'll want and need on board in order to see the plan through. The ten-year plan gives the owner a call to action. It puts the focus on prosperity rather than preservation, which is critical to growth.

"I DON'T BELIEVE YOU'RE THINKING BIG ENOUGH"

Committing to ambitious goals is emotionally very difficult, make no mistake about it. Sometimes, even with the stellar high-growth owners, there comes a time when they wonder if they're really up for the challenge.

An owner I'll call Jack underwent some enormous growth over three years, through business acquisition and truly remarkable organic growth. At that point, he told me he didn't think it was sustainable. It was time to stop growing and just work on integrating all the new acquisitions, even though he had vetted those acquisitions so thoroughly that they were proving to be no problem at all.

I got on the phone and challenged Jack with his ten-year plan. He had a vision of where he wanted to be in ten years, and now all of a sudden, he wanted to back off. Why? Jack admitted he was struggling with the idea of taking his company to the next level.

"Let's go back and look at what your track record is," I said. Jack is very analytical, and he had run all the numbers. He'd done his homework. He'd been averaging more than 25 percent growth per year for five years.

"If I forecast that out over the next ten years," I said, "you'll actually be doing higher numbers than what you'd previously thought." His trajectory was pointing toward several billions of dollars in assets under management, even though he was managing about $200 million at the time. I told Jack that it didn't really make logical sense to me why that growth would not be attainable for him.

"I don't believe you're thinking big enough," I said.

Next thing you know, there's silence on the phone.

"Jack," I said. "Are you okay?"

Silence.

"Jack, should I call someone?" I really did wonder if he'd fainted or had a heart attack.

I heard a weak voice on the line. "No. It's okay." He sounded far away.

"What's going on?"

"I'm on the floor," Jack said. "I'm curled up in the fetal position."

"Are you okay physically?"

"I'm fine," Jack said. "This hurts. This really hurts. But I need it. You're right. I'm not thinking big enough."

From there, Jack recognized that he could grow his company fifteen times its current size by sticking to his ten-year plan. He sat in front of everyone at the company and announced the goals of $100 million in shareholder equity, $40 million in revenue, and $4 billion in assets under management. That would mean he'd have to grow the company by a multiple of fifteen in under ten years.

The point is that after several years of working with the ten-year plan and then revising it annually to account for new growth and successful new acquisitions, a future possibility came into view that was so enormous it left Jack stunned and curled up on the floor. I think he panicked at that moment because he recognized that it wasn't a pipe dream or a blue-sky projection. He went back, played out the path he'd been on, forecast these astounding numbers, and asked, "Why not? Why can't we do it? We've already been doing it."

That was back in 2017. By 2020, Jack's company was right on pace to achieve its ten-year goal.

When I first started working with Jack around 2012, his annual revenue was just $650,000. It would have been absolutely inconceivable at that time to predict that in fifteen years he'd be approaching $40 million in revenue. It would have been too overwhelming. Instead, what it took was a ten-year plan and five years of solid growth. It took several seismic shifts in thinking every time big choices needed to be made, and with each acquisition, Jack grew as a person and as a leader.

It's been a tremendous privilege to see up-close that kind of growth in Jack and in many others like him. I've been coaching long enough to see people experiencing rates of growth and stepping into huge new leadership roles that they couldn't have imagined when they started just a few years earlier.

What if that were you? What if in less than ten years you could look back and see that you've achieved something you would consider impossible today? What would you need to do in order to actually exceed the limits of your own imagination?

MAKE A FIRM IMPRESSION
Three Questions

The Mindset

Try to imagine a turbo-growth goal for your company so huge and frightening it could leave you curled up on the floor in a fetal position.

The Practice

What's on your stop-doing list today that would best prepare you for enacting a ten-year plan?

The Opportunity

What obstacles are keeping you from thinking and strategizing long-term?

PART THREE

The Client Experience
Officer

CHAPTER SEVEN

Position Yourself

The third and final section of this book deals with your role as a client experience officer. You've seen how your beliefs determine your effectiveness as a chief executive officer, and how your personal values and mission define your role as a cultural excellence officer. Now you'll see how the personal choices you make, beginning with your daily attitude, are at the root of achieving self-perpetuating turbo growth. Everything depends upon finding, attracting, serving, and keeping the right kind of clients, and your personal positioning determines how well you succeed.

One of my most popular presentations begins with a story about the time I purposely booked our team into a low-end motel that's part of a famous national chain I'll call Cheap Motel. We were visiting St. Louis for two nights, so we spent the first night in Cheap Motel and the next night at the local Ritz-Carlton.

Our objective was to document each stage of customer experience at each place. With Cheap Motel, things started to go wrong immediately at the front desk. Our room reservations, priced at $39.95, were screwed up. *Oh good*, I thought. *We're going to see how the staff reacts and get an idea of what Cheap Motel calls customer service.*

It wasn't service with a smile. It was service with a sneer. The guy at the desk made us feel as though we were putting him out because someone in the reservations system had messed up. And then we had to come down to the main desk to make the changes. That surprised me. I assumed that with so many thousands of rooms to manage, the chain's economy of scale would ensure a very strong booking system. As I learned more about Cheap Motel, the reviews got worse.

Two young female assistants were sharing one of the rooms. The first thing they noticed when they entered the room was an enormous brown stain on one of the quilted bed comforters. "Yuck!" they said. *Great!* I thought, *another test for Cheap Motel customer service in our hospitality experiment.* They called the desk. More exasperation. No, the motel didn't have any other comforters they could use. The laundry wouldn't arrive until the next day. The only acceptable solution was to change rooms. So back down to the lobby we went to make the necessary changes. My two assistants quickly examined the second room and were glad to see no brown secretions on their bed coverings. Stained by the experience, though, our team members slept in their clothes that night. They didn't even want to look at the bedding under the comforter, much less sleep in it.

And as you can imagine, our experience at the Ritz-Carlton the next day was the polar opposite. The attentiveness from the staff was nearly overwhelming from the moment we were welcomed at the entrance, where the valet parking attendant knew my name. Later that day, when one team member remembered she'd left her camera in the car, we called down to valet parking and it was retrieved and delivered to our door within the hour. And guess what? The Ritz-Carlton also screwed up our reservation! One of the rooms we'd reserved wasn't available, so the Ritz-Carlton upgraded us to a suite and then gave us a discount for our trouble! The Ritz-Carlton brought up the mistake upon check-in and already had the solution ready to deliver. Their mistake and the way they handled it lived up to their reputation of being a top luxury brand.

Every Ritz-Carlton employee we met was flawlessly courteous and thoughtful. Our customer experience there was a pure expression of Ritz-Carlton's leadership approach and what the company brand stands for. The same was true of the budget motel experience. The desk clerk there didn't treat us with much respect because the motel management probably doesn't have much respect for customers. The brand identity is reflected in the $39.95 room rate and the hallway vending machines stocked with more condoms than candy. Upper management prefers strictly transactional relationships with its customers, and that was exactly our customer experience.

THE IMPORTANCE OF ATTITUDE

Throughout my day, whenever I'm asked how I'm doing, I almost always give the same response:

"Bullish on life!"

That's only one of the ways I maintain my positive attitude. Reminding myself that I'm bullish on life all through the day keeps any negative self-talk in my mind to a minimum. Even if I'm having a lousy day, this technique of talking to myself (instead of listening to my moods) is one of the best ways I've found to stay on top of my goals and uplift the people around me.

"Bullish on life!" has become part of my personal brand. I've been told by phone receptionists that they look forward to my calls just to hear me say it. And if I ever give a different reply when people ask how I'm doing, they'll often stop and ask if I'm okay.

Maintaining a positive attitude can be hard work, especially when things are not going well. Once, during a severe market correction, a friend of mine confessed he was trying to stay positive, but it was hard to find a bright spot when accounts were down. What he was missing, I told him, is that our business isn't about financial markets. It's about how we react to the markets. It's about relationships. It's about our ability to interpret the markets in a meaningful way. It's about leadership. And leadership requires a positive attitude.

I've known people who defend negative attitudes as being realistic. They are numbers-oriented people who take comfort in hard facts. They are wary of excessive optimism that can lead to reckless risk taking.

I don't endorse taking an unrealistic view of the world. In fact, I endorse the opposite. You have to understand the real issues and challenges if you are going to develop successful solutions. Intense focus on the negative can lead our brains to ignore everything else and can result in giving us a distorted perspective that prevents us from seeing things that are going well or that bring us joy. A positive attitude, one that's bullish on life, raises our thinking above this level. It forces us to widen our focus and take in the daily miracle of all the good people and good things in our lives. *That's* being realistic.

I spend a lot of time and energy keeping my attitude focused on the positive. It's something I've worked on diligently for years because it's worth it. In my coaching I can see very clearly that for most people, the biggest obstacle to success is allowing negative thinking to affect their attitude toward life.

Studies show that positive thinking expands your creativity, inventiveness, and focus on the big picture. Negative thoughts do the opposite. They prompt you to take actions that are small, narrow, and more survival based. We all know this is true if we think about it.

Everyone knows a few very smart and skilled people with bad attitudes who never seem to reach their potential.

Positive thoughts actually equip you to better deal with whatever unavoidable negativity comes along. Psychologist Barbara Hendrickson has studied the effect for years in the Positive Emotions and Psychophysiology Laboratory at the University of North Carolina. Her broaden-and-build theory of positive psychology shows how a positive attitude sets in motion an upward cycle that *broadens* your range of thoughts, activities, and relationships, which in turn *builds* your capabilities and personal resources to deal with adversity.

So, when it comes to positioning your business in the marketplace, before you make any practical marketing decisions about your niche and target market, you must begin with your own personal positioning. Take an inventory of your attitude, your thinking, your words, and actions, and take stock of what example that sets for your employees. Attitude is contagious. If you want your associates to radiate positive attitudes toward each other and toward the outside world, you have to model that attitude yourself. That's the shape of your future and your business.

A second analogy to consider is the force of attraction. Whatever you are is what you will attract. What you are not, you will repel. Attitude is just the start. People with negative or sour attitudes naturally attract people with similar dispositions. Misery loves company and so does joyfulness. Which one do you want?

Some leaders claim they like people with positive attitudes because they enjoy the lift they get from them. But have no illusions that if you are running a business and leading with a negative attitude, you will lose your sparkplugs and bright lights.

It really comes down to whether you have a Cheap Motel attitude where you treat clients on a transactional basis, a Ritz-Carlton attitude where you build long-term relationships, or something in between.

Both Cheap Motel and Ritz-Carlton are profitable companies in the hospitality sector, so from a strictly financial standpoint, each one is successfully positioned.

On the other hand, in the financial services sector, you're not going to get very far with a Cheap Motel attitude. And it's not enough to project a Ritz-Carlton attitude with clients but a Cheap Motel attitude with your team. Just as surely as your beliefs and values shape your company's operations and culture, your personal positioning shapes your sales and marketing to clients. You have to position all the dimensions of your outward presentation in alignment with the goals and objectives of your business.

To do that, you must come to grips with how you, personally, are the living embodiment of what your clients see and experience. How you position yourself personally sets certain parameters for your company's position in the marketplace. From Dr. Qubein, I have learned seven different positioning methods you can use:

SEVEN WAYS TO POSITION YOURSELF

1. **Position yourself with your attitude.** Attitude is the first and fundamental position you must consider. Do you authentically maintain a positive attitude toward life, work, and people? Here's a better question: If your attitude were for sale, who would buy it? Would they be willing to pay a lot for it? If not, why not?

   It's time for some introspection. Think of your personal skills and knowledge. Are they really so exceptional that your company naturally stands out over all the others in your market? Unless they are, it's time to consider that your attitude is what will make or break you. With so much at stake, consider all the measures it might take for you to maintain a positive daily attitude.

Meditation, journaling, and religious practices have all been shown to have beneficial effects of prompting daily positivity.

2. **Position yourself in your own mind.** Ask yourself a few very frank questions to help you assess where you stand in your market:

- Why would anyone do business with me?

- If prospective clients were in the marketplace to buy what I sell, why would they think of me first?

- Why would they think of me at all?

- Am I confident in my value and knowledge?

- How easily can someone else imitate what I do?

- What's missing that would strengthen my position?

3. **Position yourself with your appearance.** Ask yourself if your personal presentation reflects your attitude and your thoughts. Really take stock of your choices of clothing, grooming, your physical fitness, posture, and bearing. When people look at you, are they able to see how you see yourself, how you are positioned in your own mind? Does your outward appearance project your inward positioning?

Being thoughtful about your appearance is *not* about fitting in. It's not about conforming to other people's expectations. It's about projecting your personal identity in a way that attracts people you want to work with. My personal presentation is a lot like my speaking presentation: not for everyone. I've given considerable thought to dressing in a way that is not corporate but more business casual. My typical daily outfit is a custom-tailored sport coat with a button-down shirt, jeans, and cowboy boots. It's a look I call *Garden & Gun*, after the popular magazine about Southern lifestyles and culture. That's just who I am, and it's why I feel perfectly comfortable being dressed that way in a roomful of suits.

4. **Position yourself with your actions**. Consider what drives your choices for action each day. Are you engaged in business by design or business by default? Are you fulfilling expectations each day for yourself, your associates, and your clients? Or are you making choices based on sudden crises and the pressure to keep up with the competition?

    Imitating the competition rarely works, and when it works in the short term, it merely leads you away from your true goals, away from self-actualization. After years of volunteering with a local youth sports league, I've noted how a nearby rival organization keeps imitating our recruiting and fundraising methods, but to no avail. Our participation numbers keep climbing while theirs keep going down. They'd be much better off coming up with their own approaches that fit their own mission and the specific skill sets of their volunteers.

    That's just one of many examples of how information is highly overrated. There's already so much of it around that the only value is how to make sense of it and know what to use. Information becomes useful knowledge the way food becomes nutrition: the value is realized only by knowing how to choose from a vast abundance of options. Is the knowledge you offer made up of cheap empty calories or does it constitute a healthy balanced diet? If so, then you're positioned to be something more than a source of information or knowledge. You are a respected source of wisdom.

5. **Position yourself with your focus.** What is your focus in your everyday communications? Are you focused on generating income

or generating value? What comes first in your concerns: building a good company today, or building a great business in the long run? In every choice that you make, are you looking to grow the business or engender client loyalty?

More importantly, do you, as the CEO, know what your priorities are each day when you walk through the doors? Every morning before going into work, I sit at my kitchen counter and look at my to-do list. I circle the three to five things I've got to do that day to move everything forward, come hell or high water. That's my morning. If I get those things done, I can go to my secondary to-do list. But what I never do is waste time at work thinking about what I should focus on next.

All the choices you make as a matter of your personal positioning inevitably direct the future positioning of your business, whether you want them to or not. If you try to be something you're not in your marketing materials, your clients will catch on very quickly. And if you tell your associates you believe one thing while your daily habits tell them the opposite, all you will do is undermine your effectiveness and credibility as a leader. Don't think for a minute you can proclaim that your firm's growth strategy is all about generating value for clients and earning their loyalty when your team sees you frequently sacrificing those objectives for short-term gains.

6. **Position yourself with your words.** Our choices of words matter, as much as we wish it weren't so. Words reflect what we believe and what we value, so they also reflect our personal positioning.

Some words reflect your positioning in terms of relationships. Do you speak of agreement letters, or do you use more rigid, transactional terms such as contracts and retainers? In a similar way, when you speak of teaching and selling, your words betray a more self-interested position than if you were speaking of learning and serving. A document called an action plan will invite more healthy discussion and relationship building than one called a proposal even if their contents are identical.

7. **Position yourself with your planning.** Be thoughtful and intentional about how you choose to tell your story. What do you want people to learn about you? Do you think people know what you want them to know? Is your ten-year plan congruent with your daily priorities, or is there a gap there? That's what a ten-year plan is: a living document that helps you make decisions. **If you're** not positioning yourself with your plan, where are you heading?

The answers to the above questions will help you begin to understand where you currently stand in relation to positioning across the many layers of life and business. It prepares you for reimagining the kind of business you want to have.

YOUR PERSONAL BRAND POSITIONING

Usually, after I've given a talk at a big event, the organizers will follow up some weeks later by sending me their audience survey scores on my performance. I never bother looking at the results, though, partly because I'm seasoned enough at public speaking that there's not much I can learn from them. The true measure of success for me is whether the event organizers invite me to speak at their next event.

But there's another, more important reason why I don't read audience surveys. I know that with each talk I give, I'm not going to appeal to a certain number of people in the audience. Do I want to read their negative opinions? Of course not. What would be the point? If they didn't like what I said or how I said it, that's their business, not mine.

Position Yourself

I know my personal brand. It's about getting people to stretch themselves and be their best. My objective as a speaker is to challenge the audience to set audacious goals in their lives. I tell them they should consider how their personal beliefs and behaviors may be holding them back. A message like that is bound to leave a certain percent of any audience feeling irritated, because there will always be people who feel threatened or judged when you challenge their beliefs.

If I deliver that message effectively in a big room with 150 advisors or more, I realize I may be scaring the crap out of about thirty of them. But that also means that what I have to say is powerful enough to land where people feel it, where they know they are vulnerable. My message is for the benefit of the audience members who enjoy having their assumptions challenged. My objective is to engage and inspire a select few among that group who are actually ready to rise to that challenge and make big changes in their lives.

I'll never be the most popular speaker at the conference and my audience survey scores will never be near 100 percent, as they are for some other speakers. In fact, I'd be worried if someone told me my scores were that high. I'm not there to be a crowd pleaser. My messages are are actually meant to repel those who prefer the path of least resistance and mediocrity. Instead, I'm there to spark the imaginations of those who want to chase excellence. I want to connect with those who feel some discontentment in their livelihoods and suspect there must be a better way. But I'll never make an authentic connection with those people if I tailor my remarks to avoid offending anyone.

Whenever I speak, whether it's in front a large crowd, a small gathering of CEOs, or one-on-one with a client, I do my best to present myself as the living example of what our firm offers. I want to embody what we stand for. That's how I lead myself, lead my team, and represent the company to the outside world. I work hard to keep these three functions closely aligned so that when clients and prospective clients meet me, they have a direct and vivid experience of who we are and what we stand for.

Earlier in this chapter, I mentioned our little experiment comparing the customer experiences at a budget motel and the Ritz-Carlton. At the motel, we were constantly reminded how little the management cared if we were uncomfortable or dissatisfied. The motel company would be glad if we were to never go back, because customers with high standards don't fit its ideal client profile. Everything about our experience there communicated that they neither expect nor want repeat business from people who seek more than the absolute minimum in hospitality.

At the Ritz-Carlton, we were constantly reminded of how highly we were valued as guests. That's largely because Ritz-Carlton values its employees just as highly. The company educates them well about their guests' expectations. The company famously distributes little cards to its employees to remind them of the Ritz-Carlton credo: "We are ladies and gentlemen serving ladies and gentlemen."

The point is that no matter what your marketing materials say, no matter what marketing strategies you pursue, your clients' direct experience with you will give them a more profound understanding of who you are and what your firm stands for.

That's why I'll never give a crowd-pleasing talk that promises all gain with minimum pain. That's not who I am, and it's not what our firm stands for. Perhaps I'd be a more popular speaker if I sugarcoated my messaging about the high costs of self-defeating beliefs and behaviors. I might even attract more leads. But they wouldn't be the high-quality leads that are a perfect match for what I do.

I'm a big fan of the restaurateur and author Danny Meyer. I've been to his restaurants, I've seen him speak, and I've read his bestseller *Setting the Table*. "Know thyself" is one of his primary prescriptions.

Position Yourself

He writes, "It's a very rare business that can (or should be) all things to all people. Be the best you can be within a reasonably tight product focus."

Have you positioned yourself that way? You need to, whether you're ready or not. Our entire industry faces the challenge of how to remain relevant to our clients' needs in a world cluttered by commodity products and avalanches of financial information. The most valuable product any advisor can offer to clients in such an environment is a close, ongoing, coaching relationship. To distinguish yourself in a crowded marketplace, it's absolutely necessary to define your personal brand, identify the ideal clients whom your brand will attract, and then design the coaching products and experiences that best address the needs of those ideal clients.

You may already have a good idea of what makes you stand out in your local market. By positioning yourself with your personal brand power, you want to express your values so that they animate and illuminate your company's brand.

EXERCISE 7.1
Your Values in Review

Consult with your vision board and all the work we've done so far. Specifically, review your vision board responses to Exercise 1.2 and your core beliefs responses to Exercise 1.4.

- What do you value most? What is truly most important to you in life?

- In what do you consistently invest most of your money?

- What one thing do you worry about most?

- What one thing do you talk about most?

- Which of your talents have you developed most fully and relied on most often?

- What kind of challenge do you find most appealing?

- What one thing have you done in your life that you have been most proud of?

- What one thing have you done or not done in your life that you would most like to do differently?

- If you were to discover that you only had ninety days to live, what three things would you do most of?

For each of these questions, ask yourself how your personal brand expresses these values or how it *could* express them. By digging deep in this way, you have an opportunity to recognize the most personal and compelling competitive differences you bring to the marketplace. Because they are the product of your personal beliefs and values, they are powerful enough take your company to the next level of growth and take you on the next leg of your journey of personal success and significance.

ASSESS YOUR REPUTATIONAL CAPITAL

Value is in the eye of the client, just as beauty is in the eye of the beholder. In order to build value that clients will perceive and appreciate, you need to understand how others see you. The reputational capital of your personal brand is measured solely by how well your brand distinctions impact the client's perception.

For instance, you may consider that being thorough and detail oriented are important aspects of your personal brand. But if you write complex financial plans in accord with these values, you risk leaving your clients confused and bewildered. You may believe you're diligently delivering your brand promise, but your clients are getting the impression you're insensitive to their actual needs by not delivering the value in a simple, easy-to-understand format. If you can't communicate your personal brand in a way that creates value your clients can understand, your brand message has no power. You might as well not have a brand message at all.

Back in chapter 4, I asked you to take stock of your personal reputational capital as a chief cultural officer. That's because a leader's personal reputation will inevitably determine the quality of the company's culture. Now, as a client experience officer, you need to take a rigorous 360-degree inventory of how well you and your company are communicating your brand message.

You need to know what people say about you when you're not around, and what they tell others about you when they're asked. You must have a handle on where you're succeeding, where you're failing (and where you might have made no impression at all) before you can move forward in an effective and decisive way.

Ask yourself these questions about how others see you:

- **How do your clients describe you to others?** Are they getting what you offer? Or do they describe things about you that are not consistent with what you consider your personal brand? When I get positive feedback on things I've put a lot of effort into, such as creating truly special events for our clients, then I know I'm projecting my personal brand effectively.

  One client recounted how our featured guests at such events included a songwriter, a vocal coach, and a university president and then complimented me on how we'd made all those presentations relevant to financial services. That was our intention, and it was important for us to know that the client got it.

- **How do your clients describe your company to others?** When I'm speaking to people introduced through a referral, I love to quiz them on what our mutual friend told them about our company. I'm listening for signs that our clients are passing along the brand values we work so hard to project: that we are a community of advisors who are open-minded, supportive, coachable, and offer consistency and professionalism.

- **How do your employees describe you to others?** I only give tough feedback to people I care about. That's part of my personal brand. So, I give a lot of tough feedback to the coaches on our team. I do this in the spirit of tough love. But do my coaches see it that way? Is that what they tell people when they talk about me?

  If I don't ask around, I won't know if my personal brand is landing with them, or if there are aspects of my coaching that need improvement. One coach has told people he likes my tough feedback because it makes him better. Another said that she considered me a big, soft, teddy bear, and she accepted the tough feedback because she sees my kind and loving side in the workplace, as well.

  When your employees validate who you are in these ways, you can be sure that you're building reputational capital with them. If they respect and admire you for reasons that align with your personal brand, then you know you have a company culture that they value enough to share with others, including their coworkers and the company's clients.

- **How do your friends describe you to others?** Sometimes your closest friends are not delivering the message you want them to put out there. They mean well, but their perceptions might not be aligned with your brand message. It's up to you to find out what they're saying and explain to them why you'd prefer they say it differently.

- **What do people think of you before they meet you?** This is an easy question to ask in a first meeting. Is their response consistent with your personal brand? A lot of prospects tell me that the referrer advised them they should only talk to me if they're serious about growing. That's always great to hear because it means my messaging is getting through. I think of how much time I've saved over the years because almost every time I sit down with someone referred to me, that prospect is fully aware of what I offer.

- **What do people think of your company before they meet you?** I also ask this question at the first meeting. They may have heard nice things about me as a speaker, but how has that translated into what they think about the company? Is it possible your personal presentation doesn't match how people regard your company? You want to listen for evidence that your company values are clear among the people who are your advocates.

- **Do they think of you at all?** Sometimes you'll meet people you assume know who you are, but they don't. That's a handy warning signal. Ask some of your confidants why they think this happened. They may have some useful insights about why you're not better known. They may have ideas they haven't thought to share with you before. You may not like the answer, but it's important to listen. It's one of those moments where you have a choice between making something useful of an unpleasant experience or simply nursing your bruised ego in private.

You ask these questions knowing you might not like all the answers. If you are committed to turbo growth, then you'll see that the answers you dislike the most are the ones that promise you the most value.

From their responses, you have to ask yourself a third set of honest questions:

- Am I known in my industry?

- Am I different in a way that matters to my clients?

- If people are not doing business with me, why not?

- What is my strategy to overcome these three big issues: ignorance, apathy, and resistance?

The answers to the above questions will help you begin to understand where you currently stand in relation to positioning across the many layers of life and business.

They prepare you for reimagining the kind of business you want to have, and the kind of life you want to have. Because, make no mistake, the path to everything you want in life runs right through the exceptional value and exceptional experiences you provide to others.

This personal positioning sets the stage for all of your company's future growth, and all your marketing and sales strategies, the life blood of your business. These personal choices—how you think, what you prioritize—inevitably shape the ideal client profile for your products and services. That ideal client profile, in turn, is essential to ensuring that you can run an efficient and effective marketing plan that targets the clients you desire most.

POSITION YOURSELF:
Three Questions

The Mindset
What would you need in order to say that you're bullish on life on a consistent basis?

The Practice
What area of personal positioning can you work on today?

The Opportunity
What's the one thing you can do today to enhance your reputational capital?

CHAPTER EIGHT

Riches in Niches

An advisor I'll call Frank has more than seventy clients who all work at MegaCorp, a large employer in his city. He began his practice with just two or three MegaCorp employees, and their numbers have grown over the years.

With each new client he takes on at MegaCorp, the better able he is to leverage his thorough base of knowledge about the company's complex benefit and retirement plans. When he meets with these clients, Frank can point out details about MegaCorp's plans that most other advisors would never be aware of. Sometimes, after he's solved a particular problem with one client, he reaches out to his other clients at MegaCorp to let them know he's found a beneficial new option they might want to consider.

Frank has gotten to know MegaCorp's HR people, who now alert him whenever there are changes in the benefit plans. With each change, Frank analyzes the potential impacts on his clients and then sends out emails to let them know what, if anything, they may have to be concerned about. The email invites them to get in touch if they have questions, and says he'd be happy to talk to any of their colleagues who have questions about the change.

These seventy clients enjoy superior service from Frank, but they get something much more important and special: They get peace of mind. They feel that Frank is looking out for them. He has their back, and as long as they stay with MegaCorp, no other financial advisor can ever give them that same *feeling* of security.

The client experience is an emotional experience, and as a client experience officer, you're in the business of emotions management. The product you offer will register with your clients as something much more than just a product; it's a series of emotional experiences.

In that sense, what you're offering is the product *of* your product, not just the product itself. An ice cream vendor, for instance, isn't just selling cold treats. The product of his product is the feeling of relief on a hot day. He's selling happiness, he's selling memories from childhood, he's selling family togetherness. When you go back to that same ice cream vendor, it's not just for the taste of the ice cream. You're returning for the very personal emotional experience you enjoy while eating his ice cream.

Frank's story is a good example of why we say there are riches in niches. Frank's strong niche of seventy clients at MegaCorp enables him to give those seventy clients powerful and specific emotional experiences that they can't get anywhere else. Every time there's a change in the company's benefit plans, Frank's email update provides them with the comforting feeling that he's there for them, even if the change itself is of little or no consequence. The email reassures Frank's clients that nothing gets past him. And that gives them the feeling of confidence that Frank is their best possible choice of advisor. Bigger firms with better-known brand names don't stand a chance in attempting to lure away Frank's MegaCorp clients.

Frank also has built a niche among local physicians. He has so many physician clients, in fact, that he's learned the ins and outs of running a successful medical practice, from top to bottom.

When he's talking to the physicians, they treat him as a confidant because he understands the peculiarities of their business. It's the same with another client, Trevor, who's become an expert in the oil and gas industry and grown his GDC from almost nothing to almost $2.5 million in less than ten years by serving that very volatile, boom-and-bust niche.

There are many other advantages to building four or five strong niches of this kind into your practice, but this is the fundamental advantage: Niches provide you with the opportunity to offer client experiences that will be second to none. If you can execute that promise, then all your niche-marketing strategies for driving growth in your business will become more focused, more lucrative, and more fun.

ELEPHANTS AND MICE

Having worked with hundreds of top advisors, I've learned that the one thing almost all of them have in common is a very clear view of whom they are trying to attract as their next top-shelf clients. Within each of Frank's four or five niche markets, for example, he has a very clear idea of who his next clients should be. He sets minimum financial criteria for new clients, and he politely advises those who don't meet that criteria about their various options for financial planning advice. Sometimes Frank refers clients to other advisors within his firm, each of whom have their own favored niches and specific financial criteria for new clients.

Developing your own niches in this way begins with sorting out your top clients, their interests, and shared characteristics. You should be hunting for what I call elephant clients. They're elephants because bagging them can be difficult, but they are well worth the effort because they offer jumbo-size rewards. Elephants carry larger streams of revenue and deliver a higher lifetime value to you.

Above all, elephant clients tend to bother you less and value you and your time more than the smaller, pesky clients I call mice. These are clients who are very easy to attract, multiply fast, and once you have them, they can be pests. Mice clients bother you for attention and require more sales and service efforts than bigger elephant clients. Paradoxically, your mice value you less than your elephants do. You're better off without these clients, but as you would with real mice, you need to make a conscious effort to get rid of them.

Ask any business owners what they would do differently if they were starting over, and most would tell you they would work only with elephants and not with mice. But most new businesses need revenue and take just about anyone as a client. That usually means they attract a lot of mice who generate very little income but take up a lot of valuable time and energy.

If you want to start landing elephant clients and seeking the riches in niches, you've got to get rid of your mice. First, stop allowing them to eat up your time and attention, and some will go away on their own. The preferred option is to package them up and sell them to another firm, so you can capitalize on the equity you have built over the years. Failing that, you can pass them along at no charge to someone starting out, someone who's grateful for any new client, just as you once were. If there are a few mice that you wouldn't wish on anyone, you should let them go immediately.

I know it isn't easy. If you've never seen mice as a problem before, they have a way of multiplying and taking over. One coaching client of mine, someone I'll call Arnie, was able to turn around his entire practice as soon as he recognized the added value he could be creating for his best and most enjoyable clients if he pared back his numbers of mice.

The first thing we did to help Arnie with his mice infestation was to identify a profile of the type of client he enjoyed working with most. He and I dug in together on an account-by-account analysis, setting aside the consideration of profitability for the time being. We found that the clients Arnie truly liked all shared two or more of these characteristics:

- They valued his opinions,

- They acted on his advice.

- They made timely decisions.

- When Arnie met or spoke with them, he felt energized.

Most of Arnie's clients did not fit this description at all. They were mice he'd accumulated over the years when his single-minded focus was on growing his client base. They were generally poor communicators who rarely followed through on his advice. Many of them complained they couldn't afford to make the moves he recommended.

The most frustrating of the bunch tended to put off making decisions for months at a time. Instead, they kept coming back to Arnie, pumping him for more details and more information, taking up much more of his time and energy, and in the end doing little or nothing with the advice he gave them.

For the very first time, Arnie recognized that if he were to begin divorcing some of these most egregious clients, he'd have that much more time and energy to devote to finding more of his favorite kind of clients. But the process of culling his business wasn't easy. Some of these unenjoyable clients had been with him a very long time. Some he considered friends and he felt bad letting them go.

The hardest cases were the handful of high-net-worth clients whom Arnie truly disliked working with. Even though he found himself in constant conflict with them, he'd always told himself they were a burden worth bearing. He had a serious concern about whether he'd be able to replace their income if he were to sell them to another advisor.

With time, though, Arnie stuck to the plan and let go of his mice, including the high-net-worth mice. It didn't take long before their revenue had been replaced with the right kind of client: someone with both resources *and* a healthy respect for Arnie, his time, and his advice.

This is not a one-and-done exercise. For all businesses, it's an ongoing process to prune clients who no longer fit into the company's future plans. Over time, some clients will become far more trouble than they're worth, while others will no longer fit with your niche strategy.

But whatever you do, it's imperative that you stop accepting new mice today. When it comes to new clients, you want to be an elephants-only firm. Remember that elephants are scared of mice. And you should be, too.

Hunting big game naturally raises your game. To attract elephant clients, you have to see yourself as an elephant in your own right. And your team members should be a herd of elephants who show up on time, carry a passion for your business, and have the capacity to grow with you. As you attract more elephants, you'll understand them better and become more like them, which is good because it's a law of nature that like species attract like species.

In Arnie's case, to get a clearer picture of the type of elephant he wanted to hunt, he ranked his fifteen favorite clients according to annual recurring revenue. For the first time, he could see how many of his most enjoyable clients were also among his most financially rewarding. Then he sliced and diced the list of favorite clients into categories, sorting them by industry, employer, age demographic, and common interests. He also made a list of those who had referred other prospective clients to him.

Through this process, he was able to estimate the average lifetime value of his top clients, and also saw which of his potential niches were most lucrative. He wrote out a paragraph describing the desired criteria for his top-shelf clients, including minimum annual revenue, specific industry/profession, age demographic, hobbies, interests, values they operated by, and personality traits. For each niche he planned to pursue, he added why his clients in this niche category should be advocates for his practice. Simply put, if you can't articulate why new elephants should want to join your herd, you don't have an identified niche.

Elephants are difficult to acquire, even though they are everywhere in plain sight because they're so big. It takes a lot of ammunition, greater attention, and superior focus to land an elephant. Here is an exercise to help you understand the elephants in each of your niches.

EXERCISE 8.1
Your Elephants in Each Niche

- What pains do they share?

- In what ways do your products and services address those pains better than anyone else?

- What would you need to do to be considered an expert in this niche?

- What is the most efficient and effective way to communicate this message to the elephants out there?

- What hobbies, interests, and community interests does your niche like?

- What other professionals serving your niche do you need to get to know?

This exercise is also available to download from our website: dynamicdirections-d2.com/the3ceos.

Exploring all these questions is another one of those ongoing tasks that is never done. All of your niche marketing efforts rely on answering these questions as best you can. Keep collecting data, and with enough research on your niche clients, you can build a positioning, marketing and sales plan that will attract your ideal clients within each of your target niches.

YOUR MARKETING PLAN: SPRAY AND PRAY VERSUS TARGET AND HARVEST

Most top advisors typically have three to five segments of clients they enjoy working with and want to duplicate. Those three to five niches allow the advisors to develop a marketing plan for each niche that zeroes in on strategically selected activities, specific strategies, and media platforms that have high concentrations of these targeted niche clients. This is a much more efficient and effective approach than the more common alternative, derisively called spray and pray. The idea behind spray and pray is to throw a lot of different marketing activities at the public and hope that prospective clients emerge in response. It's a try-anything approach, with no defined audience, a mix of noncongruent activities, mass media campaigns, and other random techniques and strategies.

Niche marketing takes a target-and-harvest approach instead. It focuses your resources on a particular market segment (niche) that has a high potential to connect with your services. The objective with any niche is to be as narrowly focused as economically feasible so that you will enjoy a competitive advantage over advisors whose value propositions are less relevant to the clients in that niche. Niche marketing requires more concentrated practice in one area so it can really fine-tune your expertise into a tighter focus. The payoff is that it enables you to become an expert or thought leader in your niche. Most clients will pass up larger firms or better-known brands if they can find an advisor who has superior knowledge and expertise in their chief areas of concern. Niche marketing requires you to compete in smaller ponds, but with each niche you pursue, you stand a better chance of becoming the biggest and best fish in each of those ponds.

Returning to the example of Frank and his niche at MegaCorp, he grew this niche in a very deliberate way that was at once very forward and very humble. He was aware that in order to cultivate new clients at the company, he'd need the cooperation of the gatekeepers in the MegaCorp HR office. When the company introduced a series of new benefits changes, Frank requested permission to hold a lunchtime event where he could answer questions about how the changes might impact financial and retirement planning. MegaCorp's HR officers were so pleased with the event that he's now a regular visitor to the company for these events, because MegaCorp's benefits change fairly frequently.

Frank also asks each of his clients at MegaCorp for their advice on what they think he should do to obtain more of their colleagues as clients. Frank accepts each suggestion with gratitude, carefully examines the merits of the advice, and in most cases does exactly what his clients advise. Sometimes, when clients are happy to help him but not sure what to suggest, Frank is ready to solicit their opinions on some of his own approaches and strategies. We all enjoy being asked for our opinions.

The more specific your product or service, the less competition you will have for clients. When competitors can't duplicate your niche strategies and expertise, the less you have to worry about competitive pricing. You just have to choose niches wisely, and make sure they're worth pursuing. You may find that a niche market has been unattended by competitors because it's not lucrative. Before you pursue a niche, make sure there are enough elephants in it to make hunting worth your while.

Businesses that serve niche markets tend to stand out for their unique focus, whether they specialize in the retirement plan market, or work with entrepreneurs, doctors, or some other niche occupation. Professional specialties attract attention from media outlets such as blogs, websites, podcasts, radio talk shows, and newspapers. Even if there are many in the audience who aren't among your target audience, it's good to be widely known for your particular specialty.

Digital marketing, with its capabilities for audience segmentation, is ideal for niche marketing. All the research you do into your ideal client profile can pay off when the research is applied to digital marketing data and analytics tools. When you serve just a few demographics, professions, or interest groups, you have less work to do, and much less of your work is wasted on raising prospects who do not meet your ideal criteria. The key is to become well known within that very specific segment of prospective clients you are targeting.

MAKE NICHE MARKETING FUN

Every niche marketing strategy should aim at the objective of making you the dominant fish in a relatively small pond. Niche marketing is especially effective for reaching prospects who can be targeted based on common characteristics that include hobbies, occupations or belonging to civic groups and political advocacy organizations. When it comes time to plan marketing events, these very specific niches open all kinds of possibilities for creating fun that you know the members of the niche group will enjoy.

For these kinds of marketing events, you want to produce first-class exclusive offerings that strictly limit the number of clients and guests who can attend. By keeping the participant number small, you create urgency for your clients to reserve their spot as soon as possible. These small venues are most effective when you create an event that appears private and difficult to get into unless clients or guests have an exclusive connection: you.

If you look at these small group events of no more than twelve to sixteen people as investments in your business, then the kinds of memorable activity you can script for your clients run the gamut. Sometimes the most successful social event takes into consideration what the clients in your niche love to do and what you love to do. For instance, one of our clients, Michael Hancock, has managed to incorporate his passion for fine wines into very popular wine-tasting events for his clients. Thanks to his example, at D2 we refer to all kinds of niche marketing as purple-teeth marketing.

When we plan a purple-teeth event, what we're looking for is a fun, interactive experience with one of our niche clients and a few members of their community. Besides wine tasting, purple-teeth events have included cooking classes, bourbon tastings, private dining, fishing expeditions, exotic-car test drives, historic tours, and all kinds of interesting how-to events. The emphasis during purple-teeth events is purely on fun and socializing, without any sales presentations or even discussions of finance. Instead, you focus on building a deeper connection with your clients and establishing a new social relationship with your client's guests.

This is how you can create truly memorable experiences for your clients. When you put on an event that excites you personally, you'll find that you're eager to take the extra time to make invitations during review meetings. Your enthusiasm about the event will be contagious to everyone around you, before and during the event itself. You will create an event checklist and timeline to guide you and your team in creating a positive experience that builds client confidence *and* introduces you to new prospects who fit one of your niche profiles. You can simultaneously get results and have a great time getting them.

When some of the niches you serve arise right out of your interests, passions, or special abilities, that's much more than a happy side benefit. It's an essential alignment between who you are and the clients you serve. Your clients benefit from this kind of niche marketing because you are more likely to be fully engaged and passionate about what's most important to them.

I know an advisor who has built a very strong niche serving the LGBTQ community in a college town located in a very conservative area. The niche has turned out to be very lucrative, and the advisor gets to work with people he enjoys, people who in turn feel safe and secure that he understands the issues common to that very specific community. It's a force multiplier in the growth of your company when you are able to do more of what you love, and with clients with whom you share a special connection.

The eruption of the COVID-19 pandemic in the spring of 2020 presented an unusual set of challenges and opportunities for us. Aware of our coaching clients' sudden sense of isolation, we decided to be a resource for them with a series of twice-a-week Confidence in Crisis webinars. We brought them expert advice on working from home, leading remote teams, and onboarding new team members virtually, and we coached them on mental performance and conditioning and ran sessions on stress management and mindfulness. Week after week, we hosted conference calls where our clients shared ideas on which teleconferencing services were working best, how they were marketing themselves without face-to-face meetings, and any number of other unique marketing and management contingencies.

We didn't cancel our slate of events. We rescheduled them and reimagined them as virtual events, and added some new ones, as well. We hosted virtual concerts, virtual comedy shows, a virtual grilling demonstration, even virtual wine and bourbon tastings. Then we shared what we learned from these ad hoc adventures with our coaching clients so they could profit from our experience. We also went out of our way to send out more gifts than ever (out of our untapped travel budget), mostly fun and fancy foods, just to lift their spirits during a time of unprecedented isolation and uncertainty.

We received all kinds of praise and accolades from clients who were thrilled for the help we'd given them, and the spirit of generosity we had displayed. We never strayed from our usual coaching schedule or our timeline. All our Confidence in Crisis work was just added on, because that's what the times required of us during those first few months of the pandemic. The experience was a vivid reminder of how unpredictably needs and wants can change, and how important it is to pivot and adapt, and to do it with a cheerful, bullish attitude.

CREATING A REFERRAL CULTURE

A central principle of niche marketing is that getting in front of the right people is more important than getting in front of *a lot* of people. People in a niche tend to be in frequent contact with others in that niche, which means more opportunities to get the word out about your business. Word of mouth is very important to niche marketing, which means it's imperative that you work at your skills in asking for referrals.

Frank, for example, scouts around on LinkedIn profiles and recognizes who else inside MegaCorp likely fits his ideal client profile. He reaches out to his clients there with a distinctively humble request: "You have a few connections at the company who are actually the kind of people I enjoy working with. If you were me, how would I get connected with them?"

He makes similar requests in his other niches. He has a number of small businesses for whom he manages retirement plans, a niche that he's been growing with very little competition. He'll tell the CEO or head of HR, "Oh, by the way, here are ten small businesses I'd really like to work with. Do you know anybody there that you might be able to make a connection with?"

Frank believes in what he does. He has absolute certainty that his clients' contacts will enjoy meeting him and will benefit from his services. So, he works these relationships from a small set of niches, maybe three or four, all because he knows who his top clients are and he knows how to ask to get more of them, and rigorously follow through in building a culture of referral among his clients.

In general, the better you serve your clients, the more likely they are to recommend—and maybe even rave about—your services to their many colleagues. But you can't count on that. There are shy elephants and gregarious elephants. You may never get a single referral from a shy elephant, while a single gregarious elephant who appreciates you and sings your praises could help take your firm to the next level of growth.

The most common referral-related complaint we hear from advisors is that too many referrals fail to result in qualified leads. Not all top-shelf clients are comfortable opening up their personal networks to you, and that's something you have to accept. It's up to you to invest your time and energy in the clients who instinctively *enjoy* networking and making introductions.

Certain people are natural connectors. They have a special gift of bringing the world together. They are the kind of people who know everyone, and they thrive on introducing their friends and colleagues to their wide varieties of social circles. In his bestseller *The Tipping Point*,[8] author Malcolm Gladwell cited academic research revealing

---

8. Malcolm Gladwell, *The Tipping Point: How Little Things Can Make a Big Difference* (New York: Little, Brown and Company, 2000).

that connectors are easy to find in just a few steps because, for one reason or another, they manage to occupy many different worlds and subcultures and niches.

In simple terms, connectors get it. The objective of the referral tree exercise is to help you pinpoint those clients in your practice who get it and spend as much time and energy as possible cultivating these relationships for client growth.

One of the things you'll learn from being around connectors is how to become a connector yourself. I once signed a high-net-worth client after recognizing that he was an avid turkey hunter, and I happened to have a retired client who ranked among the nation's best-known makers of turkey calls. I arranged a special meeting between the two, and we wound up spending half a day together "talking turkey" at my retired client's farm. Then, on the ninety-minute drive back home, we discussed his finances. A few months later, the three of us went turkey hunting together. On the same day I bagged my first turkey, we signed the transfer paperwork for several accounts with my new client. I didn't need to share my new client's passion for hunting. I just needed to show him I was attentive to and in tune with what made him click.

You should know where your clients have come from. Review your entire client base to see how many clients each of your top-ten clients have sent you. Then list the names of each current client who can be directly connected to them. If you go a little deeper and explore all the clients who have come from referrals, you might find you have certain top-advocate clients who get it. They understand and appreciate who you are and are eager to share you with their friends and colleagues.

This list of your top-advocate clients becomes the invitation list you utilize for smaller, exclusive marketing events. (We call it the referral-tree list because of the way the referral connections branch out.) The referral-tree list allows you to maximize your efforts in marketing by ensuring you are inviting the right clients to the events: clients who understand the importance of bringing qualified candidates to your practice. This important list also tells you whom you need to take care of most in your practice.

Even if some of your top-client advocates don't meet all of your top-shelf criteria (specifically the financial criteria), you should strongly consider treating these clients as you do your top-shelf clients to reward them for their efforts that help you grow your business.

Given the fact that these clients get it, you can speak very candidly with them about bringing people to your events and asking for introductions. For example, you could say something like this:

Hey, John, I really want to thank you for sending me Joe and Tammy, Rick and Donna, and Fred and Martha as clients over the last couple of years. I really enjoy working with each couple. We have an upcoming dinner event, and I immediately thought of you as someone I would like to invite to say thank-you. I think this also might be a good opportunity for you to introduce me to the next Joe and Tammy, too. Who else do you know who would enjoy the kind of relationship we have and who are a lot like Joe and Tammy?

There's no risk of offending John with this request because you know that he gets it. He will tune right into the same referral station your dial is on without feeling any discomfort. Odds are he'll be glad that you asked and will look forward to the event.

On the other hand, it's important to test your relationship with *all* of your top-shelf clients by initiating a referral conversation with each of them. If any of them sound uncomfortable, let them off the hook gently (especially the shy top-shelf clients) by assuring them your relationship with them is most important, and you just want to make sure they know you are still interested in growing your business. If any clients indicate that they are not comfortable introducing you to friends and family, make sure they understand that the relationship you have with them has a higher priority than your cultivation of new clients. Reassure them that your request carries no pressure.

Once you have all of these concepts working for you, building a self-renewing, self-regenerating referral culture becomes a matter of step-by-step follow-through on all the opportunities ripening on your referral tree. Executing the plan is still hard work, make no mistake. But instead of fretting about a lack of leads, you'll enjoy a high ROI from all your efforts to identify and elicit referrals from your top-advocate clients.

RICHES IN NICHES
Three Questions

The Mindset
What are your top three niches most deserving of your focus?

The Practice
As a "chief exterminator officer," what do you need
to do to get rid of your mice problem today?

The Opportunity
Who are you going to ask for a referral, and how?

CHAPTER NINE

Designing the Client Experience

When you lose one of your top clients, studies have shown it probably happened for one main reason above all others: your client felt ignored. The product you provided might have been fine. But the product of your product—as defined by Dr. Qubein, this is the feeling your client gets from the experience of your product—left that client cold, lonely, and vulnerable to a competitor's pitch.

Losing clients is almost always a sin of omission. It's not what you did, it's what you didn't do. Clients might perceive a lack of timeliness or responsiveness on your part. The frequency and quality of contacts with you might have seemed inadequate. And although it's unlikely they'll hold you responsible for a market disruption, you may lose them anyway if the disruption leaves them feeling blindsided and unprepared.

Developing a robust client experience with a customized client experience timeline for each client is the best way to manage your top-shelf clients' expectations and ensure they never feel forgotten or abandoned. The timeline is a preplanned annual schedule of communications and contacts that yields a daily plan of action for follow-through. Writing up the plan gives you a chance to define and interpret the value that you want to offer your top-shelf clients, and

149

how you want to generate memorable moments for each of them on a regular basis. It also helps set the proper performance expectations for you and your team, because if you don't get the client experience right, all the other hard work you've done will be for naught.

In 2020, Paula Dougherty was named to the Forbes Top Women Wealth Advisors list. Some years back, I was coaching her after one of her top clients abruptly left her. Paula was frustrated because, to her mind, she'd done everything right, and the client should have been ecstatic about the results Paula had created for her. Through our coaching, Paula came to realize that although she'd provided the client with value, she'd never taken the time to interpret the value for the customer in a way the customer would understand.

From then on, Paula shifted gears in how she prepared for client meetings. She made sure her team had documented everything they had done for the client in advance of each meeting. Then she presented these accomplishments in the meetings, something she'd never done before, and for the first time, her clients were connecting Paula's work with the attainment of their financial security and independence, their goals, and their dreams. Paula heard them praise her as they never had before, telling her they couldn't have done it without her, all because she took the time to measure and interpret the value of her services so clients could appreciate what she had done.

This kind of preparation is the proactive response to all the natural problems that crop up in client management. In executing the timeline throughout the year, you have a chance to showcase your specific strengths in your marketplace. Clients are willing to pay a premium for valuable experiences filled with substance and meaningful activities. By providing these activities in a consistent manner, you remind them of your unique value to them and avoid the trap of competing on price.

As a client experience officer, you need to understand that how your clients experience your company's execution and culture is of paramount importance, which is exactly why this chapter is so close to the end of the book. For eight chapters, you've been building a foundation for excellent performance, strong company core values, and focused niche marketing that yields a growing list of desirable clients. All of it sets the final stage for designing and refining your client experience so your clients can stay and grow with you for many years to come.

VALUE INTERPRETATION

Before you consider how to design your client experience and its timeline, you must understand *why* your clients buy what you're selling. It's not enough to know what clients want. You need to understand where that desire comes from. Facts tell and emotions sell; you need both to succeed.

In the field of behavioral economics, it's commonly assumed that a large majority of purchasing decisions stems from the desire to avoid pain from such negative feelings as fear, shame, and envy. There's fear in the form of FOMO (fear of missing out). There's shame, which is about avoiding the pain of embarrassment. There's envy, which seeks to avoid the painful feeling of defeat. These are powerful emotions, and you don't want to ignore any of them in the course of building your firm's client experience.

Three other motivations for buying are more gain-oriented: greed, pride, and altruism. Clients enjoy rewards, they enjoy feeling smart, and most of them enjoy being philanthropic to some degree. Your client experience design should give your clients some opportunities to experience all of those emotions whenever possible.

With these six motivations in mind, take careful stock of how your product of the product is being interpreted by your clients. It's irresponsible to leave this interpretation entirely up to your clients. You must see the value you offer from their perspective.

One great way to test this perspective is to identify a few very close and trusted clients with whom you can have an honest conversation covering these points:

- Why did you hire me?

- What was the experience like?

- How do I make you feel when doing business with me?

- How does my team make you feel when doing business with us?

- What is most valuable about what I do for you?

- What should I continue to do to strengthen our relationship?

- What should I start doing to get more business? What should I stop doing?

Throughout these conversations, keep those six motivations for buying at the forefront of your mind: fear, shame, envy, greed, pride, and altruism. Everything you do should starve the first three and feed the second three.

Now see how all of this new knowledge you've gathered can be described as a new brand promise.

The brand promise of my own company, Dynamic Directions, is that every entrepreneur builds an extraordinary life and business in an innovative culture with compassionate thought leaders.

Designing the Client Experience

The brand promise reflects how you want your clients to feel as a result of doing business with you. A promise to a client is more powerful than a goal because it commits you and your team to generating certain results. Everyone has the goal of bringing clients a good return on their investment, but that's not a result you can promise. On the other hand, you can promise that clients will receive a great experience in your office, that you will return calls promptly, and that you will genuinely care for them. Even if you make a mistake and drop the ball on these promises, you also promise to make it up to them so they will still feel that you value them.

These are some examples of how the very best financial advisors make their clients feel as a result of doing business with them:

- comfortable

- relaxed

- connected

- confident

- secure

- genuinely cared for

- special

- fulfilled

- wowed

- **extra**ordinary

- bullish

- extremely satisfied

In designing your client experience, consider the analogy of the amusement park (I first learned this analogy from Dr. Qubein). You want your clients to feel all these things and never feel they have to leave you to get a portion of this satisfaction elsewhere. When you think about your amusement park, you should ask yourself what the attractions are that draw ideal clients in, keep them there, and have them coming back for more. What is the unique experience? Where is the energy? Where is the fun? Where is the wow?

Amusement parks promise total experiences, which is why they charge so much and operate at such high profit margins. You should do the same. If there are products and services your customers value that you don't offer, find a way to add them to the amusement park.

It's easy to be sabotaged by your fixed beliefs and negative self-talk in this area. There may be some products you'd prefer not to sell, for any number of reasons. I once had a coaching client who was adamant he did not want to sell insurance. He had a lot of negative thoughts about the field and sincerely thought he was protecting his clients by not offering it.

I had to remind him of the amusement park. If he didn't offer his clients insurance, they'd leave the park and go elsewhere—and just might like the new park better. More importantly, if you want your clients to feel genuinely cared for, you don't want to tell them you don't offer a service they naturally might expect you to have. This is especially true of elephant clients. Once you've built a level of rapport and trust with them, don't risk breaking that trust by telling them they need to go elsewhere for a service they'd prefer to buy from you.

Sometimes specialists who are proud of doing a few things very well can be resistant to providing other services they don't care for as much. I know one advisor who excelled at asset management, so much so that he was paid by other advisors for his help. But his passion for that one aspect of financial advising prevented him from building his practice. He neglected to provide comprehensive advice, and when he did it, he either didn't price it appropriately or he didn't build the right relationships. There was a huge hole in the fence at his amusement park, so to speak. It took conscious effort on his part, over a number of years, to seal it up.

With rare exceptions, all your products should meet the standard of being desirable, useful, scarce, and transferable.

- **Desirability.** Is your product worth having for top-shelf clients?

- **Utility.** Does your product provide solutions to your clients' challenges? Are the solutions functional?

- **Scarcity.** Do your top-shelf clients consider it a privilege to have access to your services? Have you built a sense of scarcity into your business?

- **Transferability.** Can you effectively communicate your product or service to others? We go to experts in a particular field because they have their knowledge in order. Make sure yours is in order so people will realize your expertise and value.

These four concepts, which spell out DUST, are essential to creating the emotions in your clients that will keep them close to you. I have met many practical-minded specialists who will claim that they meet these criteria but also admit they're not sure whether their clients appreciate just how special and scarce their products really are. In other words, they are focusing on the product instead of the client's interpretation of the product (the product of the product).

Advisors of this kind rarely realize what a bind they're putting themselves in. They're setting themselves up for losing valuable clients who have a chance to properly experience the value being created for them. Both sides lose when this happens.

It's the difference between Hershey's and Godiva chocolate. I can attest that both are delicious chocolate products, and both have won awards for being delicious. So why does $30 buy about six pounds of Hershey's chocolate and less than half that much of Godiva?

The answer lies in product of the product. The product of the product for a Hershey's bar is generally utilitarian. It's a quick chocolate fix you can find just about anywhere. Delicious, yes. Special? Not at all. It's great for a quick bite on the go.

With Godiva, the product of the product is an entire experience reserved for special occasions. Yes, Godiva chocolate has a richer, more complex flavor profile than Hershey's, but that's not why it costs twelve times as much per ounce. Godiva makes sure you know how special it is in every sensory way possible. The rich-looking boxes are designed to be delicately opened, unveiling a masterpiece so attractive you would take time to admire and take in the Godiva much like a finely blended red wine: the swirl, the sniff, the drink, the swish, and the swallow.

Women know this very well. For example, if you were to ask women about the difference between receiving Godiva versus Hershey's, they would probably tell you if they receive Hershey's chocolate as a gift, it's usually masked with wrapping paper, a cute coffee mug, and a small teddy bear. However, if they receive a reward of Godiva, look out! It could be a lights-out experience!

So, if you suspect you're producing Godiva-quality work and providing Hershey's-quality presentations, ask yourself these questions:

- How am I packaging myself and my services versus the competition?

- What perception does my target audience have of me and my services?

- If they could, would my clients happily want to give my services to someone else as a gift?

- Do I have the capacity to solve complex problems and deliver on my brand promise?

- When my customers unwrap me and my services, is there substance and integrity?

Most businesses I've seen offer a mix of Hershey's and Godiva experiences. What's common in our field is Godiva-level smarts and talent wrapped in client offerings that resemble Hershey's. It's natural that you and your product are much better than your packaging, because the packaging more often involves areas outside your expertise. Go out and get web design, interior design, and marketing help from people who are as good in those fields as you are in yours.

That's the valuable lesson to take away from Godiva: if you want clients to seek you out, it's important to have an attractive wrapper, or they'll never even open the box.

If you're hunting elephants, you can't present yourself as a proud, utilitarian, no-frills Hershey's bar. That's the path of commoditization and doom. You must strive to offer Godiva-level or Ritz-Carlton-level service, because those brands most likely reflect the lifestyles of your ideal clients. You want to design your client experience so it not only retains your ideal clients but also inspires them to proudly refer you to their friends and colleagues.

FIRST IMPRESSIONS

In a typical week, I conduct about sixty coaching sessions, which means I get to make about sixty calls to frontline reception desks. When I call, I'm listening for what is said in the greetings, but I'm mostly listening for how those greetings make me feel. Sometimes I'll get the distinct sense of low energy, or of someone who doesn't want to be there that day. The greetings might be terse, or clipped, or just not warm.

I always tell the advisor about my experience. I'm not interested in getting anyone in trouble, but I want to drive home how teaching basic phone skills is one of those things you can control in your business. There's no excuse for the person answering your phones to not deliver on your brand promise by making the caller feel comfortable, confident, relaxed, secure. Your clients have a right to expect their phone call to make them feel the same way they feel when they call the Ritz-Carlton or any other high-end, luxury service provider.

The same goes for your website and your social media presence. The client's experience of your firm's offerings through each of these avenues should exactly reflect your brand promise. For most of your prospective clients, online impressions of how your company presents itself are more important than the look and feel of your physical offices. If your website doesn't function properly, make it a priority to fix it, just as you would fix malfunctioning plumbing or electricity in your office. If your social media sites don't express the right tone to attract your niche clients, find a better writer and/or designer.

When it comes to the reception area at your office, your choices of decor and amenities should use the typical Ritz-Carlton lobby as the standard for quality. Would the Ritz-Carlton have plastic wastebaskets? Would there be a stack of boxes left near the door? Would there be posters on the wall instead of original art? Of course not. Would the room smell good, with daily fresh flowers? A menu of available snacks posted? Hot and cold drinks available, served in branded mugs and glasses? Yes, yes, and yes.

When you consider the feelings you want to arouse in your clients, you want to make sure that your messages and appearances reflect your core values, communicated by your brand promise. All the work that you've put into understanding your personal beliefs and commitments, building your company culture, and curating your specific positioning in the marketplace should be expressed through the way your phones are answered, the way your digital footprint is displayed, and how your office looks and feels.

THE CLIENT EXPERIENCE TIMELINE

By developing a well-thought-out client experience timeline, you are ensuring that each top-shelf client is receiving a high-quality, predictable, and consistent experience of your company. From an operational standpoint, the client experience timeline sets the expectation of what your team will provide, who will accomplish the task, by when, and by whom. Much as the audience of a theatrical production should never see what goes on backstage or in between scenes, the show your practice puts on should flow effortlessly and execute flawlessly.

Through the development of the client experience timeline, you will effectively be creating a daily manual for your team to follow. Each stage and activity in the year-long timeline designates tasks, the team members responsible for each task, and the time by which it's to be done. It's an internal action checklist that ensures the client experience is properly staffed and executed with great consistency.

Within your top-shelf client base, it's best to determine on a case-by-case basis the number of annual meetings necessary for each client.

Then choose windows of several weeks or months during which you will be holding these meetings. By setting aside a handful of weeks four times per year for client meetings, your team gets highly practiced through repetition, as meetings are conducted one after the other. You and your team will be more focused as a result and you'll establish a groove where you and your team are satisfying a client with very high expectations.

From there, you can refer to your marketing plan to insert marketing events into the timeline along with your client event schedule. For each event, include an event planning checklist for the month before and after so that all the preparation and follow-through tasks are noted, along with who does what and by when.

In order to further deepen your connection with top-shelf clients, you should keep the client experience alive by staying in touch between scheduled review meetings. A regular set of these touches should be built into the timeline so that they are not forgotten or put off. Consistency and regularity are the effect you're going for.

Here are some good ways to let these clients know you are thinking about them:

- holiday cards

- birthday gifts

- anniversary gifts

- themed gifts for your highest-tiered clients

- client-approved investment reports on a selected investment

- market outlooks and economic viewpoints authored by approved research providers

- articles and books about travel and hobbies

- articles and books about the nonfinancial aspects of retirement

- brochures outlining the benefits of new services and products you offer

- a periodic newsletter about your practice that includes features on your clients and team members

- occasional check-ins, such as simple "How are you doing?" calls performed by a team member other than you

On a more customized level, you can deliver specific articles, books and/or small gifts on specific items of interest for a select few of your top-shelf clients. Your very best clients deserve that extra level of attention.

When sending out all these cards and gifts, never forget the lesson of Godiva versus Hershey's: the packaging can be as important as the gift itself. If the packaging and presentation lacks care and thoughtfulness, it could be worse than sending nothing at all.

After helping one of my advisor clients put together a touch program for his top clients and prospects, I asked him to add me to his list so I could monitor his mailings and provide him with feedback.

The very first item arrived in a plain manila envelope, with a typed (not handwritten) mailing label. The return address didn't have the advisor's company name on it. Inside the envelope was a small book accompanied by a poorly photocopied form letter with my name inserted at the top. There was no sticker on the book cover to remind the recipient who sent the gift.

Today, after getting my feedback, that same advisor sends out gift books in nice, padded mailers featuring company branding. Inside, there's a personal handwritten note on attractive stationery. The book itself has the advisor's name and contact information on one of its first pages, along with a company-branded bookmark.

Take a hard look at everything you send your clients. Step-by-step, consider their experience of opening and viewing what you've sent them. They're thinking of you in those moments. If you haven't given much care or thought to what you've sent them, it's likely that your carelessness and thoughtlessness is what they will be thinking about.

CREATING WOW

Back in 2008, a few years after he'd started as president of High Point University (HPU), Dr. Nido Qubein assigned one of his administrators to be the school's director of wow. Nido wanted one person on staff to be accountable for creating everyday experiences on the campus that would give that wow feeling to students and to visiting parents considering sending their children to HPU.

The result has been any number of innovations, big and small, that distinguish HPU in ways beyond its excellent academic reputation. Laundries in the dorms are free. Dorms have concierge desks for picking up dry cleaning and making wake-up calls. Along campus walkways, soft classical music plays from speakers in the flower beds. There's live music at lunch time every day. When parents schedule a visit to campus, a parking space is set aside for them with a lighted screen that welcomes them by name.

These are simple touches that don't cost very much, but they make a memorable impact on the students and their parents. From a practical standpoint, Nido says that having beautiful facilities filled with wow touches helps keep HPU's young people "on campus and out of trouble."

You want to have a similar effect on all your clients and prospective clients. You want to keep them with you and uninterested in going elsewhere. You do it first and foremost by delivering on your promises, but then you must consider the wow factor. How can you package and present your services in a distinctive way that creates that sense of wow?

And then there's the other side of the coin. Where inside your client experience are there un-wows: dreary or unimaginative processes and procedures that are either unnecessary or needlessly unattractive? What can you do to get rid of them or at least spruce up their appearance? If you have someone on staff with a talent for noticing these bothersome details, consider assigning that person as your own director of wow.

Client meetings, events and all preplanned customer touches should be rethought for their wow potential. And while it's important to systemize ongoing touches with clients through other avenues of communication, you don't want these touches to feel routinized and perfunctory from the clients' perspective. That's where a little wow analysis of each touch can be useful.

For example, you may want to send out birthday cards to your top-shelf clients. In order to execute this strategy, a team member would screen for birthdays coming up for the next month, have birthday cards presigned by the advisor or the entire team, and then mail the cards five days before the clients' birthdays.

You should also incorporate giving gifts to your clients to celebrate special moments and to reward such positive behaviors as making introductions for you. For instance, you could send a predetermined gift to a client who sends you an introduction that converts to a client.

As you decide on sending gifts, think in terms of systemization by sending the same gift for the same occasion and the same behavior you want to reward. Empower one of your team members to pick a couple of vendors to determine a packaged gift so all you have to do is provide the personalized message for the gift and the address to the vendor.

One financial advisor struck a deal with a gift basket company to send out a packaged gift each time a prospect converted to a client. The first package was customized by the advisor and then the gift basket company developed a checklist of items to be included in all future gift baskets. When a new client came on board, a designated team member would instruct the gift basket company where to send the package, with a card attached to the gift.

You want to show clients they're appreciated by giving them gifts with sincerity, and a handwritten note is a simple gesture that goes a long way. Personalize gifts whenever possible to make them more meaningful. Find a gift source that will allow you to add monograms, names, and logos to your gift items.

Gifts at major holidays tend to have less impact because holidays are when clients are inundated with other gifts. Sending "just because" gifts pack an element of surprise and deliver on the true wow. It's not necessary to break the bank purchasing client gifts, but keep in mind that your top-shelf clients probably have top-shelf taste. Segment them out so you can splurge on high-end gifts where appropriate.

And then there are recovery gifts. Everyone makes mistakes, and you should have a process in place for how to respond when you or your team screws up. Someone may miss a meeting or forget a task, or any number of little things can go wrong. Look at it as an excellent opportunity to build more trust and intimacy with the client. Simply acknowledge and own the mistake to your client, apologize, correct the mistake, and then follow up with a recovery gift.

A handwritten note to the client could say something such as "I apologize for our mistake in scheduling your meeting. We value you as a friend and a client. Please enjoy some coffee on us! Apologies again for the inconvenience. I'll see you at our next meeting!" Then insert the date of the new meeting, along with a $10 gift card to a local coffee shop. Make sure the gift is appropriate to the client and the size of the mistake. It's the thought that counts, and the execution will gain you much goodwill with your clients. They may just repeat the story to their friends and help build your reputation among potential clients.

THE CLIENT EXPERIENCE LETTER

An annual client experience letter serves to outline what your top-shelf clients can expect from you over the coming year. Some advisors send out two letters each year as a best practice: an annual early-spring letter and a follow-up autumn letter that provides end-of-year tax advice and new events announcements.

The annual letter should contain an outline of all the services and events described in the client experience timeline. The client event schedule informs them of whom they may bring to each event, the number of clients and guests who can attend, the date, time, and location of each event, and a compelling message describing the event. The client event schedule will be attached to your client experience letter.

The letter should also include everything you plan to provide in order for you to leverage the concept of surprise and delight with clients. When composing these letters, place yourself in the role of an advertising copywriter. The goal is to produce an exciting narrative that will guarantee you sell out each event. For optimal results, and if writing of this sort is not one of your strengths, consider finding a capable team member to draft the letter, or outsource this critical task to a professional.

The letter is one of the most important communications you will send out. It functions as a promise to the client, and to your team. It spells out the expectations of top-shelf clients, giving you a benchmark to formally measure your relationship and the promises you make on your end.

THE CLIENT MEETING

A lot goes into the preparations and follow-though surrounding each regularly scheduled client meeting, but the important point is that the chief function of the meeting is to deliver the product of your product, the feeling that your client is well taken care of, feels lucky to have you as an advisor, and is eager to help you build your business.

Aside from all the regular items to go over during the meeting, you should also have a special theme for each meeting whether it's a long-term-care insurance campaign, a benefits assessment, a will and trust check-up, or an overall estate-planning check-up. It's very easy to fall into a rut if you provide the same presentation and agenda with each quarterly meeting, so the special theme can add a spark of spontaneity. It will enliven the conversation and make the entire session feel fresh and more memorable for the client.

In the meeting itself, you want to review what you've done with the client together as a team. This is not a rundown of what you've done for the client, although the client will certainly get that message. Instead, you want the client's interpretation of events to be focused on what you have achieved *together*. The first time you do this with clients, you want to capture all of the specific actions they have taken to enhance their financial situation with all the supporting details. Then you should document the value they received from you in a follow-up letter. Each time you meet after the first time you interpret the value, you should consider bringing up the value that has been rendered since the last session.

It's important to be prepared for these meetings, but not so well prepared that it sounds like scripted rotework. As the young concert pianist Daniil Trifonov once said, a performance should reflect "rigorously prepared spontaneity." From my own background in theater, I've learned that if you know your character well enough, it's not a calamity if you drop a line or if your opposite onstage goes off script, because you know how your character would react.

The format of the meeting is fairly simple. If you've been my client for ten years, I may go back and list all the things we've done that have contributed to your financial success. I'll point out what an amazing journey you've been on, and how, when we started out, you weren't happy with how your finances were organized. But look at them now! We've done an estate plan, you have retirement goals, and we've saved you tens of thousands of dollars in taxes through all that work.

I might start off the summary by saying how proud I am of you, how you've done this hard work that not many other clients do. If you're set to retire earlier than anticipated, I'll recognize you for that accomplishment. In that moment, I want you to feel your own glory.

And then from there, I'll humbly ask you if I've missed anything in our working relationship, if there's anything I could be doing better. The result almost always is that the client will thank me and say that none of this would have been possible without me.

That's a great thing to hear. It means I've achieved maximal value interpretation. My clients express in a heartfelt way that they recognize the value I've brought them.

Achieving that euphoric moment, as we call it, is the top nonnumerical goal you're striving for with every client. It's a great moment for resetting the relationship, to pivot to the opportunities in the years ahead, to raise the possibility of buying new products in line with those plans.

It's also a perfect moment for requesting referrals, because it's in the context of merely asking the clients to share with friends and colleagues something they've just recognized as highly valuable in their lives: you.

SUSTAINING SUCCESS THROUGH THE TIMELINE

Building a robust client experience of this kind, when executed faithfully through the year, helps you articulate your value proposition and its unique differentiating advantages. Just as a Godiva chocolates box does, the packaging of your client experiences enhances the level of enjoyment by your top-shelf clients and makes it easier for them to bring you referrals. Why? Because an attractively presented set of consistent and reliable experiences is fun to talk about. Some of your clients will brag about you to their network of friends, family, and colleagues, because having found you makes them feel smart.

The design of your client experience timeline should be so sound that when speaking to potential clients, you don't need to pitch your services in sales mode. You can simply ask the prospects a few questions about their current financial advisor.

"How comfortable are you with the way your current advisor presets your quarterly meetings for the year?"

"How do you feel about the detailed follow-up letters you receive after each meeting, and how they outline what was discussed? "

"Do you enjoy receiving the advisor's follow-up items?"

"How do you feel about the regular contacts concerning investment updates, even when there's nothing to sell?"

"Do you enjoy the regularly scheduled client appreciation events?

Asking these questions will prompt prospective clients to reflect on their current financial advising services, and most will react with disappointment or dismay. The vast majority of your competitors are not providing this kind of client experience, and even in the rare cases where they have somewhat similar services, those services are not likely to be presented in such an appealingly cohesive package.

The prospects will have questions for you, and the feelings your answers will arouse in them will be all the negative emotions known to drive purchase decisions: the fear of missing out, the envy of those who have it better, and the embarrassment of having second-rate service. Behavioral economics tells us these simple questions, based on your client experience timeline, will drive these top-shelf prospects away from their current financial advisors and into your client base.

DESIGNING THE CLIENT EXPERIENCE
Three Questions

The Mindset
What can you do to enhance your brand promise today?

The Practice
What can you do today to make your company more Godiva and less Hershey's?

The Opportunity
What's a wow experience you're able to give a client today?

CHAPTER TEN

Commitment or Regret: The Choice Is Yours

According to a Greek legend, Milo of Croton was a wrestler who built his immense strength by lifting a calf on his shoulders every day until eventually he was lifting a fully grown bull.

That's not a widely recommended weight training regimen. But what I like most about Milo's story is the power of his commitment. He lifted the calf *every day,* even as the task grew larger by the day. And as he did, his confidence grew each day that he was up to the task that he would face the following day.

That's what the concept of the three CEOs demands of you. As you keep to the tasks in your ten-year plan, your capacity to handle your ever-growing scope of control will keep expanding right along with the size of your company. Staying with that discipline is not only vital to succeeding in your plan for growth but will awaken in you your natural ability to make and keep strong commitments. Your awareness of the power of commitment will help you build belief in yourself and your abilities.

The great business author Jim Rohn once said that we all must suffer one of two things. Either we suffer the pain of discipline, or we suffer the pain of regret and disappointment. When your commitment to anything is too weak, when you fail to take proper responsibility for what needs to be done, regret is the inevitable outcome. So your choice each day is to endure the momentary discomfort of executing on your strong commitments, or to allow your weak commitment today to weigh you down with regret tomorrow.

One of the most common regrets that CEOs experience is when they take too long to remove a team member who doesn't fit with the company culture. In most cases, even the troubled team member knows it's not working long before the ax falls. But I've seen even the best CEOs put off the inevitable parting until it's almost unbearable. Then once the problem is gone, they hear from the team all the stories of just how much toxicity that one employee was generating. They feel regret that they'd failed to live up to the ideals of the company's culture.

Short-term regret of that kind can perform a positive function in our lives. Regret can help remind you of what not to do again. It pokes at your conscience, and the pain might provoke some insight as to how to avoid a similar situation in the future. It also reminds us of the price of our passivity. Every child has to get singed at least once by a hot burner on a stove top before learning to stay away from the burners. The pain of regret can raise awareness of our need to change our behavior.

Longer-term regrets, built up year after year, have a much greater hold on us. Lost opportunities get stuck in our craw. In the past, we behaved in a way that brings us shame just thinking about it. Maybe someone's gotten hurt because of our actions, and there's a sense of unfinished business that haunts us about what we did. *If only.* Woulda, shoulda, coulda.

Back in chapter 1, I told you how Dave Mazzetti was driven so hard by outward goals and achievements that his regrets were beginning to pile up. He wasn't present in many of his personal relationships. He'd built a lake house for his family and had no time to spend with them.

He'd gained a lot of weight, almost as a physical manifestation of his regrets. Dave was able to transform his relationship with regret only when he was able to reorient his focus to living from the inside out. Today, he remains as focused on growth and success as he always was. But he's no longer overwhelmed with regret when he falls short of his goals. He knows there are more important things.

Unresolved regrets are toxic. Make no mistake about it: If you are carrying these regrets with you, it will be difficult, if not impossible to achieve turbo growth, no matter how hard you try to work through the exercises in this book. In my experience, obsessive lingering feelings of regret rank among the top reasons why certain advisors never reach their potential.

Deep-seated regrets undermine the faith it takes to adhere to your strong commitments. Simply put, regrets are dream killers. They can make you feel old and worn out long before your time. The famous actor John Barrymore once commented that "a man is not old until regrets take the place of dreams."

Barrymore recognized the one-to-one relationship between dreams and regrets. If you don't pursue your dreams today, you will regret it tomorrow, along with all the pain that comes from knowing what you've missed. Your dreams never die. You either pursue them through your commitments or you take them to your grave in the form of regrets.

In every phase of this journey there are landmines of regret for not having begun this work much sooner. Inevitably you'll have feelings of "if only I knew then what I know now."

The exercises on your fixed beliefs and self-limiting beliefs will inevitably arouse some sense of regret for your not having been aware of them sooner, before they had a chance to limit your progress and potential. Building your company culture anew may well remind you of the years you've spent saying yes to too many things. Everyone feels regret at the number of "mice" they've accumulated over the years, and how they've postponed the pain of paring them back. And of course there are regrets related to the client experience when you start executing a more robust client experience and inevitably feel bad about not implementing a client experience timeline much sooner.

I know a lot of people who avoid talking about their regrets because they're embarrassed by them. What they miss is how discussion can offer enough perspective and distance from regrets that you can learn from them and set them aside. The healthiest approach is to picture your regrets as you would outdated inventory. Regrets may be cluttering up and crowding the warehouse of your mind, where all your fresh thoughts and innovative ideas should be easily accessed. No responsible business owner allows stale old inventory to crowd out the the new popular stuff. That's why every retailer has an end-of-season sale to make sure unpopular products are out of the warehouse to make room for the new products.

You need to hold a fire sale of your old regrets. Try writing out the major regrets in your life and describe how each one happened, and who might have been hurt besides you. Then make a companion list of major accomplishments and milestones that make you proud, and what you did to make them happen. For both lists, make note of the role of commitment in each.

Now it's time to unload the stale inventory. Share the list with your coach or confidant, someone you can trust to receive these regrets without judgment. As you go over the list, make note of the weak commitments that caused you regret and the strong commitments that resulted in accomplishment. Write out a few sentences describing each so you can see the connection clearly. Make a list of the people who benefited most from your achievements.

The final step is to take note of the people you still regret having harmed. Make a commitment to yourself and your coach or confidant that you will apologize to them. In most cases, you'll find a simple "I'm sorry" is all the other person needs to hear. Reliving the details of the event helps no one. In most cases, both of you are ready to move on.

You may feel such apologies are not necessary, but they are. Taking responsibility and promising to change your behaviors is one of the strongest motivators you will ever find. When you let go of the excess inventory of regret inside your head, you'll find in its place all this new, clear space in which to think, plan, and dream.

Once you move past your regrets, you will see what you had presumed were limits on your life fade into nothingness. I've seen it happen time and time again, in my own life and in the lives of my coaching clients, and it's never as difficult as it may seem at first. As a coach, I get frustrated when I encounter people resisting or putting off this simple exercise, because I've seen in the faces of others the expressions of relief and joy from this exercise. I've experienced first-hand the amazing feelings of freedom that it offers.

The most successful owners we work with are also among the best at processing their regrets. They don't hang on to regrets for very long, and they're good at finding ways to resolve them. It's a mental attribute that helps them excel as executives, because the job of CEO is to always be moving forward. You face adversities, you solve problems, you confront mistakes and failures by learning and making adjustments. If your eye is perpetually on the possibilities ahead, there is no time or energy to waste dwelling on what might have been.

You've gotten this far in the book because you believe in yourself enough to know that there is a better life available to you. Don't cheat yourself by skipping some of the exercises in this book or by only skimming the questions at the end of each chapter. Keep this book handy as a reference tool that you consult regularly. Download the additional resources from the D2 website and don't hesitate to contact members of the D2 team for additional guidance. Your ability to keep to strong commitments has gotten you this far. Now you have a golden opportunity to take those abilities to a higher level as you cast off the ball and chain of lingering regret.

Once you give yourself permission to chase your dreams at full force, there is little that can stop you from achieving turbo growth in your business and achieving significance and fulfillment through every aspect of your life.

Commit yourself to change. Move on to a new season in your life with a positive attitude and stronger determination to accomplish the vision laid out on your vision board. Following through takes discipline, but the results are powerful and well worth the effort.

The choice is yours. Which direction will you take?

COMMITMENT OR REGRET
Three Questions

The Mindset

What pains of commitment do you need to suffer today
so you don't suffer the pains of regret tomorrow?

The Practice

What is your biggest regret and how can you move past it?

The Opportunity

What is really stopping you from pursuing your dreams full-force today?

Acknowledgements

Books are not written alone, and *The 3CEOs* is no exception. Thank you first to my mentor and coach, Dr. Nido Qubein, for being such an inspiration to me in all aspects of my life. My life changed immeasurably for the better since I met Nido, and I'm so grateful for his almost two decades of mentorship and how he's helped guide me to my own path of significance.

Thank you to my long-time business partner, Drew Watson, who supports my endeavors with cheerfulness, a "Totally, I got your back" attitude and a sharp analytical mind. We have accomplished a lot together, and the best is still to come.

Thank you to the creative team who helped me put the book together. Noel Weyrich provided structure, editing and writing insights, while Ben Hoak helped manage the project. Bill Williams, Steve Barger, Bill Cates, Lester Matlock, Joe De Sena, Drew Watson, Bill Young, Dr. Zach Gerbarg and Greg DeHaan were gracious to read the manuscript and provide valuable feedback.

Thank you to my Dynamic Directions team for pursuing excellence in our work together. The stories and concepts in this book are a result of what we do every day in our service to others. I am truly blessed to be surrounded with such inspirational, high-integrity, and innovative team members.

Thank you to my amazing D2 clients, who allow me to help you pursue your dreams. None of this would be possible without you, and I'm grateful for the trust you place in me and our firm.

Thank you finally to my family. My wife Christy's support is way more than I deserve, and I know I am a better person for having you in my life. I want to thank my children Ryland, Lucy Jagoe and Stone, as each of you bring out the best in me along with providing an immense amount of joy.

—Travis Ray Chaney

About the Author

Travis Ray Chaney is the CEO of Dynamic Directions (D2), a coaching and consulting firm focused on building an extraordinary life and practice for financial advisors. A Certified Master Coach®, he has coached clients to places on the *Barron's* Top 1,200 Financial Advisors list, the *Barron's* Top 100 Female Advisor list and Forbes list of Best-In-State Wealth Advisors. As an entrepreneur, he also owns multiple other businesses in different industries.

He is a former award-winning financial advisor who consistently ranked in the top 1.5% of financial advisors at his broker dealer. Travis is also the author of *Turbo Growth: Proven Strategies to Create an Extraordinary Life and Financial Planning Practice.*

Travis lives in Owensboro, Kentucky, with his wife Christy, son Ryland, and daughters Lucy Jagoe and Stone. He is a bourbon enthusiast and a country music songwriter.